Discipline That Develops Self-Discipline

MADELINE HUNTER

University of California, Los Angeles

CORWIN PRESS, INC.
A Sage Publications Company
Thousand Oaks, California

Other publications by the same author:

Mastery Teaching
Motivation Theory for Teachers
Retention Theory for Teachers
Teach More — Faster!
Teach for Transfer
Aide-ing in Education
Improved Instruction
Improving Your Child's Behavior
Parent-Teacher Conferencing
Mastering Coaching and Supervision

Discipline That Develops Self-Discipline
© Copyright 1990 by Madeline Hunter

Printed in the United States of America.

Hunter, Madeline C.
     Discipline that develops self-discipline / Madeline Hunter.
          p.   cm.
     ISBN 0-8039-6317-3
          1. School discipline — United States.   I. Title.
LB3011.H887   1995
371.5 — dc20   95-7958

For information on the complete Madeline Hunter Collection, please contact:

 CORWIN PRESS, INC.
A Sage Publications Company
2455 Teller Road
Thousand Oaks, CA 91320-2218
Call: 805-499-9774 Fax: 805-499-0871

98 99 00 01 12 11 10 9 8 7 6

To my family who survived it, this
book is affectionately dedicated

CONTENTS

FORWARD

Psychological knowledge that will result in significantly increased learning, both academic and behavioral, is available to teachers. In many cases, however, this knowledge remains unused because it is written in language that takes an advanced statistician to decode, or it is buried in research journals in university libraries which teachers have neither the time nor the energy to locate.

This book is one of a series* written to make that important knowledge available to the classroom teacher. As such, it makes no attempt to achieve comprehensive coverage of the subject, but endeavors to interpret knowledge which is most useful in the daily decisions of teachers. The purist in learning theory may complain that some generalizations are over-simplified. Our answer would be that understanding a theory in simple form is necessary to the desire to search for increasing ramifications and complexities. The reader must also be warned that decisions based on learning theory are decisions of how to teach. The decisions can be made only after the teacher has made decisions of what content to teach and which objectives are appropriate for each learner in that content area.

In other words, once a teacher has identified an appropriate educational destination for the learner, knowledge of learning theory will reveal the most effective, efficient and economical route to reach that destination. To this route, once identified, the teacher will add his or her own artistry.

Appreciation for their teaching is expressed to my early professors who made psychological theory meaningful to me, and to those professionals who encouraged me to translate theory into language and examples which were meaningful to teachers who were enhancing instruction from preschool to post doctoral students.

My greatest debt is to those students, teachers, administrators, and colleagues who constantly push me into learning more and more about "discipline which develops self discipline."

Gratitude is expressed to Christine Carrillo Miner, Cathy Dandridge, and Sarah Kincaid for their assistance in decoding and typing this manuscript.

* For information, TIP Publications, P.O. Box 514, El Segundo, CA 90245.

CHAPTER I
SELF DISCIPLINE: OUR PRIMARY OBJECTIVE

To be productively, comfortably, and responsibly in charge of one's own behavior is the hallmark of a mature, self actuated, productive person. All discipline should be designed to achieve this goal, as nearly as possible, with every student.

Our dignity, which is our feeling of being competent, valued, and in charge of ourselves, is one thing we humans dread losing and will try to maintain at all cost. Consequently, when we help a student maintain control of his/her own behavior, both of us are working towards the same objective. When our actions cause a student to lose the dignity of being in charge of self we are working at cross purposes, and all that student's skills (and they are considerable!) will be used against us.

When we discipline for self discipline, we convey the following messages to the student:

"You are in control of your behavior and therefore are accountable for it."

"You are in control of making choices within an acceptable range."

"You are competent to make these choices wisely."

"You are responsible for what happens as a result of your choice."

All of these messages convey that students can control their own destinies and that you respect their ability to do so: they are valued and competent. These messages don't have to be elaborate or complex. They can be as simple as:

"Let's meet to plan ways so you can get your work finished."

"You don't seem to feel like working now. If you prefer, you can finish it during recess (or after school)."

"Which consequence do you think would work best to help you remember?"

"Are your parents helpful when you have a problem? Would you like them to come to school and help us work on this one?"

Notice there is no question of letting students get by with poor behavior. The parameters are set by the teacher but the student is given the responsibility for selecting the best solution to the situation even if it may be "lesser of the evils."

How to establish and maintain self discipline is the number one concern of all beginning teachers. Unfortunately, it remains a concern of teachers who have not been taught basic principles of human learning or who have not intuitively stumbled onto techniques that are effective in producing self discipline while they maintain students' dignity. The result from lack of these professional skills can be confrontations and humiliation of either or both student and teacher with resultant hostility, frustration or even despair.

It is regrettable that in teacher education there is such a gap between what is now known about cause–effect relationships in students' learning self discipline and what occurs in classroom practice. It is to narrow that gap that this book is written.

A critical attribute of any professional is the skill of enabling a client to function without that professional; to be in charge of self. A physician is successful when the patient is cured and can maintain health. An attorney is successful when the case is won or the document is drawn so the attorney no longer is needed. An architect is successful when people enjoy the building so much they don't want to move.

So it is with teaching. A teacher is successful when the student no longer needs the help of a teacher in order to perform productively. That performance may be intellectual, social, emotional or physical. In this book, we will focus on students' productive self discipline, but the same principles of teaching and learning work just as effectively to produce academic, social, emotional, artistic or physical achievement. Responsibility for using social influence on the behavior of others, so they work to achieve a productive goal for themselves or for others, is the hallmark of leadership in any field.

The student behavior with which we deal in school usually is not genetically based, but is learned behavior. Anything that is learned can be taught and teaching is our business. Therefore, let's examine how we might combine the science of human learning with the art of teaching to achieve students who are self disciplined: have achieved cognitive control of their own behavior. Self discipline means that rather than ''conforming'' or ''knuckling under'' to authority, students are electing to behave in a way that is productive and brings them satisfaction. An analogy is the difference between the person who wants candy but resists it and the person who has learned to prefer fruit for dessert. Productive behavior can become preferred behavior. This goal is not always achieved in discipline or in nutrition, but it's one toward which we strive.

In the last two decades, we have learned more about the brain and how it functions to guide behavior than had been learned since the beginning of time. Much of what we learn reaffirms our experience and previous research. Some new research, however, suggests ways that are more effective than our previous practice. Another hallmark of a professional is that the person never stops learning new skills and, as a result, becomes increasingly proficient. So it is with teachers in achieving students' self discipline.

This book will focus on research based theory and translate it into teaching decisions that produce effective classroom practice. There is nothing more practical than good theory which identifies cause–effect relationships between teaching and learning. There is nothing more useless, however, until that theory is understood and implemented by thinking, decision making educators. Research based knowledge, well thought out decisions and intuition are all essential to artistic performance in education.

There are no "rules" in teaching. There are "principles" which, when applied appropriately (at the right time to the right student), can dramatically increase the probability that the student will learn to be productively in charge of self and no longer need the presence of a teacher in order to act responsibly and accountably.

Physiological psychology, behavioral psychology, social psychology, and cognitive psychology have all made their own unique contributions to our understanding of learning and behavior. To argue which psychology is "correct" is to argue whether your right or left leg is more important in running. You need them both! In the same way, we need all branches of psychology. In this book we will use research from all four branches, from reinforcing productive responses to the successful utilization of neural energy which results in the self direction of metacognition and dialectical thinking.

Researchers must keep their work environment "pure" in order to produce valid knowledge. Practitioners (teachers), however, use any combination of research that will produce the desirable results of self disciplined students. It would be impossible to use only one branch of psychology and be a successful teacher. In the same way, an architect must use many types of architecture, a physician many types of medication if either is to work successfully with all clients.

To reduce bulk in this book, no attempt will be made to cite specific research studies for each generalization. Those sources can be found in any beginning psychology text. Let's begin (not limit!) our skills with century old research that we are continuing to refine and extend: reinforcement theory.

The minute most people hear the word "reinforcement" they conjure up slobbering dogs, pecking pigeons, M and M's or token economies. That is as far removed from artistic, classroom use of reinforcement theory as is opening a can of beans to culinary art. If you are starving and don't know to cook, open the beans, but *learn* to cook. If the only way you can get students to behave productively is to bribe them, do it, but *learn* more effective professional skills which result in students becoming productively in charge of themselves. Start right now!

When reinforcement theory is mentioned, many teachers conjure up visions of a Skinnerian laboratory with rats pressing bars or pigeons pecking. "Children aren't rats" is the common way of dismissing all "that laboratory nonsense" from the procedure of the classroom (Remember, however, that most break-throughs in medicine begin with animal research).

Those same teachers, when questioned about problems of the teaching profession, will list students' behavior as their number one frustration. As they go on to describe this behavior: "They don't come in quietly," "I can't get their attention," "The only way Joe solves a problem is by fighting," "Susie won't even try in math," the sophisticated listener recognizes behavior problems that a little reinforcement "know how" could go a long way towards solving.

While it is possible to introduce very complex dimensions of reinforcement theory, the understanding of, and ability to prescribe and implement four simple principles will make all the difference between a chaotic classroom and one in which most students are responsibly in charge of themselves. While these reinforcement principles are deceptively simple to understand as statements, they are incredibly complex to implement in high speed, artistic performance. In the same way, it is simple to *explain* where to place a finger and how to use the bow on the violin. It takes years of practice, however, to play the concerto in the appropriate tempo with artistic interpretation. Excellent teaching is an artistic, action performance behavior, a performing art such as music, drama and skilled athletics. While the musician, dancer or actor knows in advance exactly what to do, the athlete, surgeon or teacher starts with a plan but must make high speed adjustments on the basis of unanticipated data emerging from people and situations. As a result, skills must be practiced to the point of split second decision making and automaticity in their implementation. It takes a great deal of thoughtful, guided practice to reach this degree of professionalism and requires continuing *coached* practice to achieve virtuosity in performance.

So, give yourself time to really understand the principles outlined in this book, practice making daily, research based decisions about which principles to use with your students in a particular content and situation, then practice implementing your decisions to the point where you can execute them artistically at high speed while teaching.

Let's begin with one of the most powerful principles governing our behavior. Whenever we do something that works out well for us, there's high probability we'll "do it again." Notice that with humans we're always working with probability, never certainty. When the physician prescribes medication it is with the probability that it will be effective. There is no certainty.

As an example of this first principle, if you go to a new restaurant and have an excellent meal at a very modest price, the next time you go out to eat there is high probability (but no guarantee) that you will return to that restaurant. You will "do it again."

If you need a new outfit and at a certain store you find exactly what you want on sale for half price, the next time you need clothes where are you apt to go? It's pretty obvious isn't it? It's just "common sense". Remember, with humans, there is no guarantee. Behavior that is reinforced simply becomes more probable.

Making "self discipline" more probable is the goal of effective and artistic teaching!

CHAPTER II
POSITIVE REINFORCEMENT

The first principle that we can use to create self disciplined students is *positive reinforcement*. A positive reinforcer will strengthen the response it immediately follows: make that response more probable or more frequent. To predict what might be a positive reinforcer we look for something a student needs or desires.

Now "stimulus" and "response," may be words to which the reader has been negatively conditioned (no doubt by a poorly taught psychology course that dealt with Pavlov's salivating dogs). Consequently, for the purposes of our discussion we will substitute a student's behavior for the word "response" and what happens after his behavior, which can be what the teacher does, as the "reinforcer" which produces "positive reinforcement." Thus when John, after working diligently, hands in his math paper, the teacher says, "You really worked hard to get it just right. You should be proud of yourself!" Handing in the paper is the response and the teacher's compliment is the positive reinforcer. Saying those words when John hands in his math paper will increase the probability that he will do it again: result in positive reinforcement.

Stated in psychological terms, when a positive reinforcer ("You really worked hard!" etc.) *immediately* follows a response (handing in the math paper), it strengthens the response and increases the probability of reoccurrence of that response (John will be more likely to hand in his paper next time because he got approval, which he desired). A positive reinforcer should follow *immediately* to result in positive reinforcement. Saying "good for you" after a lapse in time will not accomplish much.

Reinforce means "to strengthen." We reinforce a behavior to make it stronger, which means to increase the probability or the frequency of that behavior. "Stronger" in the behavioral sense means that reinforced behavior is more apt to occur than some other behavior, or that the reinforced behavior occurs more frequently than it did in the past.

"For him, intelligent decision making is more probable than is tossing a coin," means that intelligent decision making is a more likely or a more frequent behavior than is coin tossing. It does not mean that intelligent decision making always occurs or that coin tossing never occurs. Another analogy might be, "Bill will probably play better than others." This does not mean that Bill always wins over another player, but if you're betting money, your best bet is Bill.

The technical language for this "common sense" principle is, "Whenever a behavior is followed by a positive reinforcer. That behavior is strengthened: made more probable or more frequent." The reinforcer is the cause, reinforcement is the effect. A positive reinforcer is defined by its results. A positive reinforcer increases the strength of the behavior it immediately follows. Therefore, you can't say, "It didn't work" because if it didn't strengthen the behavior, it was not a positive reinforcer.

Positive reinforcement results from something desirable being added (+) immediately after a behavior occurs. If that "something" is needed, pleasant or desired by the person, it is highly probable the behavior will be strengthened. Johnny says, "Please, may I?" Mother says "Of course you may, you asked so politely." Johnny's polite asking will become more probable or more frequent. If Johnny whines and fusses to get his way and mother "gives in," whining and fussing will become Johnny's more probable or frequent response. The behavior, asking politely or fussing, which is followed by getting what he wants, will be the behavior that is strengthened and will occur in the future with greater probability.

To simplify our discussion we will use "positive reinforcement" to indicate that a response has been followed immediately by a positive reinforcer.

We could diagram reinforcement as follows:

Behavior + Reinforcer = Reinforcement (becomes stronger)

When we say a less desirable behavior is "weakened," we mean that behavior has become less probable or less frequent than some other behavior. When a teacher says, "You get the next turn because you raised your hand," (s)he is attempting to increase the probability or frequency of hand raising and decrease the probability or frequency of calling out answers or sitting without participating. Notice that reinforcement merely changed the order or probability of the three responses:

Raising hand _____ + Reinforcer   Highest probability
Calling out _____ Less probable
Sitting without participating _____ Less probable

All three behaviors started out at the same strength. When hand raising was reinforced, it became stronger (more probable). Although the other two behaviors may remain at the same strength, in comparison they now are weaker in probability than is hand raising. Reinforcement changed the order of probability (strength) of the three behaviors.

Let's look at another example. Sally usually whines to get what she wants. Whining is more probable than asking "Please, may I?" Mother has decided she wants to strengthen the more desirable behavior of asking. So, whenever she says "Please, may I?" Mother gives her what she wants (adds positive reinforcer). As a result, asking politely becomes more probable than whining. Asking has been positively reinforced (strengthened). Later we'll explain why knowing how to use a schedule of reinforcement will enable mother to keep Sally's asking behavior stronger without giving her whatever she wants for the rest of her life.

Let's translate this technical language into teaching behavior. When students are learning to behave productively, that behavior needs to be reinforced: to work out well for the student and to result in needed or desired consequences.

Applied to school behavior, this means that when a student is on time, studies, works carefully, brings required materials, listens, is polite, is cooperative and considerate, and those behaviors bring satisfaction, those behaviors will be strengthened (increase in frequency or probability). In the same way, when a student makes a smart remark to get attention and (s)he gets attention from the teacher and / or from other students, when a student doesn't bring materials and gets out of work, when a student is late and avoids the boredom of administrivia at the beginning of class, when an unsuccessful student misbehaves and as a result people think (s)he's "bad" rather than finding out (s)he's unable to do the assignment, all those behaviors are securing results that students prefer, and, therefore, those behaviors are being reinforced and consequently strengthened.

Knowing this aspect of the science of human behavior enables teachers to use that science *with artistry* in teaching to effect "preventive discipline" by deliberately seeing that productive behavior produces satisfaction for students and unproductive behavior does not!

As a classroom example, Mary is working hard and finishes her assignment. The teacher compliments her with, "You've done a great job of sticking to a hard task and finishing it. You should be proud of yourself." If Mary enjoys the compliment (and most students do), the probability of her working hard to finish the next assignment is increased.

The psychological cause–effect principles are simple. It's the implementation which involves "how?" "when?" and "why then?" that determines professional competence and artistry.

Let's see how well we have explained this.

1. We use a positive reinforcer because:

a. It will make the student more comfortable

..................................Turn to page 12 (a).

b. Teachers become pleasant people

..................................Turn to page 12 (b).

c. It will strengthen the response it follows

..................................Turn to page 12 (c).

d. A positive approach is always better

..................................Turn to page 12 (d).

a. You said we use a positive reinforcer because it will make students more comfortable.

It usually does that, but so could giving them pillows or leaving them alone and not expecting learning. There is a more important reason for using positive reinforcers. Go back to the question on page 11 and select a more defensible answer.

b. You said we use a positive reinforcer because teachers become pleasant people.

It may do that or they may blow their tops in frustration because they have to act like things are going well even when they are not. There is a more important reason for using positive reinforcers. Go back to the question on page 11 and select a reason you think is more important.

c. You said we use a positive reinforcer because it will strengthen the response it follows.

You're doing excellent thinking! (Positive reinforcer — we hope! We won't know until we see if your correct answers continue. We want to strengthen your response of making correct choices.) While there are all sorts of wholesome side effects, the primary reason we use positive reinforcers is that we want to increase the likelihood of the response reoccurring. We want the student to "do it again."

Now turn to page 13.

d. You said we use positive reinforcers because a positive approach is always better.

Usually it is, but not always. You will learn why as you read further in this program. There is a more important reason for using positive reinforcers. Go back to the question on page 11 and select a reason you think is more important.

CHAPTER III
TYPES OF PROBABLE REINFORCERS

While we never know whether our responses to students are reinforcers until we see the results, we have to anticipate what might be a reinforcer and use it deliberately in order to strengthen behavior. To do this, we can consider three types of probable reinforcers.

1. Positive messages from a significant other.

Teachers are "significant others" for most students (although high school students would rather die than admit it). Friends and family are also "significant others" but we can't control their responses. We can, however, completely control our own responses so we will focus on teachers' and principals' messages.

The message which has the highest probability of being a powerful reinforcer conveys three ideas, "You're competent, you're worthy (valued), and you've put forth effort." The importance of reinforcing effort is the result of recent research in attribution theory. When a student feels success is the result of effort, rather than ability or ease of task or luck, that student is more motivated to put forth effort again and feel in charge of and responsible for success. We know that most (not all) achievement is the result of effort. Effort is the only factor a student completely controls, so whenever possible our message needs to identify the effort put forth as well as the success that effort produced. "You really worked hard on that assignment and, as a result, you're successful," places that student increasingly in charge of self."

While we would like "virtue to be its own reward," that's not the way virtue begins. "Virtue" can result in unsatisfactory feelings. If I wait my turn, I don't get immediate satisfaction. If I let you choose first, you may take what I want. If I do my homework, I may miss desirable leisure time activities. If I raise my hand rather than blurting out, I may not get to give my answer.

"Virtue" (preferable behavior) first needs to be paired with a more immediate satisfaction. This can be accomplished by adding the social reinforcer of a teacher's positive message. These messages are most powerful if they are not anticipated by students so are surprises to them. "You are really considerate to give your friends time to think," when a student waits, or "You worked hard to get finished. Now you have free time."

Eventually, pairing of the message with a student's own feeling of being "virtuous and noble," plus success and social acceptance, become internal reinforcers that maintain the behavior without a teacher's message.

Examples of messages which indicate the student has put forth effort are: (1) positive comments on students' verbal contributions ("You must have been thinking deeply to come out with that insight"), (2) comments on quality of performance ("That's getting better and better"), (3) accepting contributions by smiles, nods, listing on board, (4) comments on following directions ("You really listened carefully to be able to do that"), (5) using a student's work as an example, without the student's name (check with the student in advance as to whether (s)he wants to claim it later) ("Let's look at this excellent paper"), and (6) private, not public, recording of productive behavior ("The record shows you've turned in your homework every day this week").

Additional examples of feedback (reinforcers) which could increase effort, feelings of competence and worth are:

"You certainly are able to get started quickly."

"You must have put a lot of thought into such an excellent introductory paragraph."

"I know you're ready to answer, you're considerate to wait for the rest."

"You don't even need reminding about your materials."

"Your hard work really paid off. That's excellent."

"That's an effective way to reorganize your notes."

"You're always on time so we can start promptly."

"That's a very perceptive comment. You're really thinking."

"You're getting a lot faster (more accurate)."

Reinforcing messages written on students' work have the same effect and can be savored and shared with family or friend.

Examples are:

"You always think to add a creative twist to your story."

"You have a real flair for adding interest with personal examples."

"You did excellent thinking to discover that solution."

"You worked carefully and got every one right!"

14

"Be sure to show this to your parents so they can see how much you have learned."

Note, that the above examples contain the message, "You are competent, respected, and your success is the result of effort." If success is not yet attained, reinforcing the effort that should eventually result in success will increase the probability that the student will continue to put forth effort.

Along with identifying effort, reinforcing messages have two other important attributes. They are precise. First, they indicate specifically what was effective rather than being general and "fuzzy" endorsers of who-knows-what, such as messages of "Good" or "Fine work." Specific messages link the reinforcers with certain behaviors rather than leaving it to the guesswork of "what caused what?" "You made an excellent choice of words so the reader could experience the situation."

A second critically important property of growth evoking reinforcers is that they are expressed in terms of "you" not "I." Note the difference in the message, "I like the way you are working" vs. "You are working so productively, you'll soon have a great _____ ." The former state-ment conveys the message, "You're pleasing me," which is not the job of the student. The "you" message builds self esteem. It conveys, "You are competent, respected and your effort will make you successful." These are the students' attributes and feelings we wish to reinforce.

There are times when an "I" message may be appropriate. However, "You work hard and learn quickly. It's fun to be your teacher," is probably more effective than, "I really enjoy teaching you."

Reinforcing messages also may be sent non-verbally. The way we look or what we do can be a reinforcer of student effort and behavior. Facial expressions of approval, nods, hand signals of, "Right on!" accepting a student's contribution or writing it on the board all convey the message, "You are competent and of value to our class."

Unfortunately, we also can send unintended messages by a fleeting look of annoyance, exasperation, body postures of boredom, disinterest, indifference, turning away or ignoring a response. These teacher behaviors are just as powerful messages even though they may not have been the information intended.

Successful teachers, like actors, learn to make their bodies "say" the intended message regardless of real feelings. Should you think this is an indication of insincerity, examine other professionals' messages. Regardless of prognosis, if the physician believes an optimistic stance will rally the patient's effort, the physician delivers the optimistic message. Even if the architect believes the client's design is ghastly, the architect works to cause modification of the plans rather than giving a candid opinion. Profession-alism involves delivering the message most enabling to the client regardless of the professional's personal feelings.

Anonymous reinforcers are a powerful way of sending a message to all students who feel it fits their behaviors. "Almost everyone is ready" reinforces those who are and alerts those who aren't. "Now everyone is ready," reinforces those who took the hint. No names have been mentioned but a lot of productive behavior has probably been reinforced.

"One person knows — two, three, four hands are up. Come on, the rest of you!" will probably reinforce those whose hands are up. You have acknowledged those who know, so they're not so tempted to blurt out the answer. The rest are warned that you're not going to let them "retire on the job" but are going to wait until they "get going." Of course, you're not going to wait forever. Before you call on someone, you might precede it with, "When I call on someone, decide whether you agree and what you might add to the answer." This keeps everyone listening, thinking, and continuing to participate.

When you indicate a particular learner, "Mary has already started working." you are running the risk of Susie thinking, "What about me? I've started too." It is usually (not always) better to say, "Some people have already started, they really know how to get to work!" Both Mary and Susie will feel reinforced. If you want to make sure Mary gets the message, give it to her with your eyes and smile so she knows you noticed her or commend her privately. Again, your thoughtful judgments about student and situation are more accurate than can be anyone's, no matter how skilled, who is not in the situation, but add anonymous reinforcers to your repertoire of skills. You'll be amazed at their effectiveness.

Positive messages from a significant other are one of our most powerful reinforcers and continue to be a reward for productive behavior throughout life. The world beams approval on people who are behaving responsibly and contributing to their own and others' success.

Privilege reinforcers

There is nothing in education (or medicine) that works with everybody. Consequently, sometimes we need to use the reinforcer of privileges: something valued that is not routinely accorded to everyone. Whenever possible, the privilege should be related to the behavior that earned it. Hard work usually results in finishing, with the reward of leisure time. Doing it correctly should result in not having to continue to do the same thing again. Helping someone often results in someone helping you when you need it. When we use privileges as reinforcers, we should endeavor to make them the privilege that would most naturally result from that behavior. Students consider it a privilege to be excused from homework because they have demonstrated competence, to socialize or make choices because they have finished work, to participate in activities because they have established or maintained eligibility.

It is important that students perceive the privilege as a privilege, not as a chore or additional duty. Some students like to help the teacher, be the chairman, do a different assignment, straighten or organize materials. Others see it as one more chore. The former see the privilege as a symbol of recognized competence, worth and effort which reinforces the effort required to obtain the privilege. Note, however, that if "politics," flattery, bullying, lying, or cheating obtains the privilege, those behaviors will become more probable or more frequent. Most of the "ills" of the world are the result of undesirable behaviors bringing results desired by the people who manifested them. In school the same unintended reinforcement results when an answer is accepted from a "blurter-outer," the student who doesn't want to be in class gets himself/herself "kicked out," the flatterer gets a better grade, or the "excuse maker" gets out of work.

Tangible reinforcers

Because the first research on reinforcers began with animals and humans with pathology, many people associate reinforcement theory with M&M's, food, tokens, or other tangible reinforcers. When one realizes that even animals respond to a warm praising voice or petting, it is obvious that social reinforcers are powerful, and most of the bribery, which passes for reinforcement theory, is not needed. Occasionally, when concrete reinforcers seem to be the only thing needed or desired by the student, we will use them (We all work for extra money which is a generalizable reinforcer). Most of the time, however, social reinforcers and privileges are sufficient.

In a few difficult cases we will need the power of concrete reinforcers, but, as in medicine, let's not use "surgery" when it's not necessary, for there could be a lot of side effects which may not be desirable.

Tangible reinforcers are those which have "physical being" and can be kept, shared with others, consumed or used. Occasionally, it may be necessary to use tangible reinforcers with the very few students who do not respond to messages or privileges. The best of these tangible reinforcers are symbolic of the behavior that earned them. A positive note to the student or, when appropriate, to his/her parents, can identify the specific behavior that "brought on" the reinforcer. Usually, such a note is treasured and saved. The author has had many students, parents, and teachers comment, years later, that "I still have the note you sent me."

The next most symbolic tangible reinforcer is a record of each occurrence of productive behavior. Records of growth (private charts, check lists) are tangible evidence of results which convey the message of a student's worth and competence. Less pounds as measured by a scale are a tangible reinforcer for a person who is trying to lose weight. Number of papers completed, arrivals on time, correct responses all constitute a desirable, tangible (can be kept and, if desired, shown to others) reinforcer. This device is used by Weight Watchers who *elect* to join the group, weigh in and record pounds lost. At school we can record on a visible chart *total* class success (*not* individual's records which should be private) number of periods or days with no tardies, no late assignments, no stops of teaching or learning for behavior problems, no arguments, no blurted out answers, whatever class behavior needs to be strengthened. We also can do this strengthening of behaviors for an individual who should design and construct a *private* chart on which (s)he or the teacher records instances of the particular behavior being successfully learned.

A warning here; *public* charts which compare students' success, *unless those students have chosen to compete*, are unfair and an invasion of privacy. The world at large does not have a right to our record of success and failure unless we choose to reveal it. Class charts which compare individuals for books read, papers turned in, tardies, etc., are a violation of productive and artistic use of reinforcement theory. *Private* records are excellent visual representations for the individual of his/her growth or the lack of it.

Awards also are tangible reinforcers but, often, they are not as immediate or as specific as needed, especially for new behaviors which need strengthening by immediate reinforcement.

Tokens to trade in on desired objects or privileges, food, or money (which is the most generalizable reinforcer) are used *only as a last resort* with students who don't respond to anything else. Because those reinforcers are not symbolic of the behavior to be strengthened, they can reduce intrinsic motivation where "doing it" is the goal, and encourage the extrinsic motivation of "doing it" to earn the reward. The motivation becomes "getting the reward" and the focus is on that reward rather than on the feeling of being responsibly and productively in charge of self or on the satisfaction of a job well done. Self perpetuating reinforcers are the enjoyment experienced from learning, helping, knowing one is correct, surprising self by creativity, problem solution, self control, mature behavior, doing a good job as a result of effort, feeling noble about ignoring an irritation or rudeness. All of these behaviors build the reinforcer of a feeling of competence which results in self esteem.

Discipline that results in self discipline requires that teachers be on the alert for productive student behaviors and reinforce them initially by verbal and/or non-verbal messages (and if necessary privileges) that signal, "You are valued, competent and are putting forth effort." Later, students will not need these external reinforcers. Their own good feelings, having been paired with productive behaviors, have high probability of maintaining those behaviors. Each of us usually feels good when we are doing the "right thing." For all of us, however, an occasional positive message from a significant other enhances our feelings of being valued and competent. These reinforcers maintain our resistance to the occasional "temptation" of less productive behaviors. It works the same with students.

Now we come to the part that is relevant to teaching. Whenever students behave in a way that we want them to continue, *immediate* positive reinforcement will increase the likelihood that they will keep on doing it. Most of us would agree with that statement, yet our daily teaching behavior does not follow it. We usually operate on the assumption that behaving correctly is only what students *should* be doing, so we ignore it. Instead of doing something (adding positive reinforcers) so students will continue that behavior, we do something about it only when they behave in a way they should not be behaving.

Let's look at an example that is all too typical. Bill comes into the classroom boisterously, obviously with no intention of settling down to the learning task. We do something! The next day he again comes in inappropriately. We do something again! On the third day, when he comes shouting into the room, our patience has ended and WE DO SOMETHING! Bill is convinced we mean business, so on the fourth day he comes in meekly and settles down to avoid the "SOMETHING." Thank goodness, we think to ourselves and proceed with the lesson. The next day Bill had reverted to his old behavior. Why shouldn't he? When he acted appropriately (came in quietly) we did absolutely nothing to increase the likelihood that he would continue to act that way, so his old habits took over.

19

We've all had the experience of a certain student always blurting out the answer, thereby spoiling the lesson for everyone else (and our disposition for us). We insist that he raise his hand. He does and we figure it's about time. Because he has already taken so many other people's turns and blurted out so many answers, we don't call on him but call on someone else. Now that we have him quiet, we feel it's only fair to give someone else a turn. On our next question he again blurts out the answer. This is probably because:

a. He has had the habit so long it will take time to get over it

. . . . Turn to page 22 (a).

b. He has never learned to take turns

. . . . Turn to page 22 (b).

c. We did not reinforce the behavior we wished to reoccur

. . . . Turn to page 22 (c).

d. He is mad because we did not call on him

. . . . Turn to page 22 (d).

a. You said he had the habit so long it will take time to get over it.

No doubt it will take a long time. However, he will never "get over it" if he tries a new behavior and it does not turn out well for him. Suppose you tried a new recipe and it was a fizzle. You would not keep on using it, would you? Turn back to the question on page 21 and apply what you have read about strengthening desirable behavior.

b. You said he has never learned to take turns.

You are a good detective but this does not help you know what to do about the situation. As a teacher, your deduction must shed some light on the kind of action that might solve the problem. Turn back to the question on page 21 and apply what you have read about strengthening desirable behavior.

c. You said we did not reinforce the behavior we wish to reoccur.

You are doing an excellent job of applying what you have read. (We hope this is a positive reinforcer.) If a student is anxious to speak and gets to do it when he blurts out and not when he raises his hand, what do you expect? We need to call on him the first time he raises his hand to be sure he will repeat an action that worked for him. Obviously, we cannot continue to call on him every time he raises his hand from now on, but we will find out how to deal with that situation in a few minutes.

Now turn to page 23.

d. You said he is mad because we did not call on him.

No doubt. But we're mad too because we have had to put up with his behavior for a long time and this is the first time it has happened to him. Nevertheless, he tried raising his hand when he wanted to speak and it got him nowhere. Turn back to the question on page 21 and apply what you have read about strengthening desirable behavior.

CHAPTER IV
SCHEDULES OF REINFORCEMENT

We have already indicated that students will not need the teacher's reinforcers the rest of their lives but will often (not always) find the productive behavior satisfying. Let's look at how we can increase the probability that this desirable outcome occurs.

Continuous schedule of reinforcement

When students are learning to elect to use a new behavior or a behavior they know but seldom use, that behavior needs to produce satisfying results *every single time it occurs*. This has not happened in the past or that behavior would be the preferred behavior. Consequently, the teacher needs to use a continuous ("consistent," "regular") schedule of reinforcers not just a "hit and miss" response. Each time a student raises a hand it should be acknowledged if that new behavior is to replace blurting out. Each time the student finishes work, comes in on time, waits for a turn, does homework or whatever is to replace less productive behavior, the desirable behavior needs to be reinforced. A continuous schedule of reinforcement makes for fast learning. Soon the new, productive behavior should become stronger (more predictable) than the old, undesirable behavior. Then the reinforcers can be spaced farther and farther apart so eventually the student will consistently manifest the replacement behavior without a reinforcer; be self-disciplined.

Intermittent schedule of reinforcers

After the new behavior is reasonably predictable, reinforcers are not necessary each time. A teacher should skip a time when a student demonstrates the desired behavior, reinforce the next time, skip two or three times, reinforce the next time, skip reinforcing increasing numbers of the occurrence of the desirable behavior until only a very occasional reinforcer is necessary to maintain the more productive behavior. Intermittent reinforcers make for long remembering and result in very durable behavior.

To witness the power of reinforcement theory, observe the slot machines at Las Vegas. A person puts in a dollar, pulls the handle and twenty dollars come out, what does the person do? Pretty obvious, isn't it, that a positive reinforcer encourages a person to "do it again." After a person has "learned" to play the machines, just an occasional win (intermittent reinforcement) will keep that person playing.

A grand master in chess told the author she had become a champion because of reinforcement theory. Her father taught her to play and at first, always let her win (continuous schedule of positive reinforcers). Then, occasionally, he would win (intermittent schedule). As she gained in skill, he increased his winning until they finally played in earnest and she won only when she played more skillfully than he. As a result of his reinforcers and her ability, she continued playing to become an international champion.

In school, the teacher needs to reinforce consistently when students are learning to practice new, more productive behaviors. As a result, there will be many reinforcers at the beginning of the school year or when students are learning a new activity. Then the teacher needs to change to an intermittent schedule so just an occasional reinforcer will maintain the desirable behavior.

As an example, the teacher might prompt hand raising by "Don't say anything but raise your hand if you know the answer to _____ . Great, everybody is raising hands and remembering not to say the answer until called on." Before the teacher's next question, (s)he prompts by, "I know you will remember to raise your hand for this one." For the next question there may be no prompt but a hearty reinforcer. "You people are great, no one forgets to raise hands." From then on, just an occasional reinforcer should maintain hand raising with most (not all) of the students. There are some exceptional students and times this strategy won't work, but we'll learn how to deal with those situations later in this book. Remember, however, the reinforcer (the desirable outcome) is in the eyes of the student and fits the age and maturity of the student as well as the circumstances of the situation. What is just right for a high school student could be all wrong for a kindergartner.

Decisions regarding the schedule of reinforcers are usually made unconsciously by the teacher depending on mood, how much the behavior irritates him/her, or personality factors relating to consistency. It is unfortunate that this is so. These decisions should be made at a conscious level for they have direct bearing on the rapidity with which students learn a new response and the ease with which they forget it and return to their old behavior.

A continuous schedule of reinforcement or reinforcing a response every time it occurs makes for fast learning. Saying "You always come in like a _____ grader," or something "complimentary" every time Bill comes in quietly will achieve the new behavior rapidly (all other things being equal, of course). His forgetting curve will match his learning curve, however, so if you completely stop reinforcing him, his good behavior will be extinguished just as rapidly. Then, "What's the use," you say — only too often all your efforts in teaching are for naught. Here is where changing schedules comes in, so that his response will be resistant to forgetting. You now need to use an intermittent schedule of reinforcers so you do not reinforce his coming in every time, but reinforce intermittently. For example, after he has learned the behavior you might reinforce the first, third, sixth, and tenth in a series of ten responses. An intermittent schedule of reinforcement will make behavior persistent and resistant to forgetting. As in Las Vegas, we always think the next time we may get the "pay off."

Let us look at tornado Bill's behavior again. For several days now, he has been coming in quietly in the morning, from recess, from noon, and from physical education. You have reinforced him every time — in fact, he now looks expectantly at you for praise. You decide you are no longer concerned with his learning the response, for this has been accomplished. The problem now becomes how long he will remember it when you are busy with other students and not around to praise him. So you decide to switch to an intermittent schedule of reinforcement This is the value of theory, it tells you what might be productive rather than your having to reach helplessly into a what-can-I-do grab bag.

Now you have a plan for Bill. When he comes in quietly you give him an especially hearty positive reinforcer. ("Bill, you just never forget to be in charge of yourself.") After recess, when he comes in appropriately and looks to you for approval, you are busy putting the math assignment on the board — with the eye in the back of your head watching Bill carefully. If he follows the usual pattern, he will look disappointed, but settle down. After lunch you will be conspicuously watching (to eliminate any possibility of his returning to his old behavior) and reinforce him with, "You just don't need a teacher at all. Why, even when I'm busy with something else, you know what to do!" That ought to hold him without additional reinforcers for the rest of the day (Remember the words of your reinforcer match the age and maturity of the student.)

The next morning you heartily reinforce him again. (Spontaneous recovery of the old behavior may take place overnight.) This time you might be able to wait until afternoon dismissal and terminate the day with, "Bill, you've come in perfectly all day today without my even looking at you." Before long, you can pretty much forget you ever had to worry about Bill being a tornado. Occasional reinforcers will maintain the strength of his behavior and the intermittent schedule will develop resistance to forgetting.

To see the change from a continuous to an intermittent schedule, let's assume that (|) is the desirable behavior and (+) is when that behavior is reinforced. An effective schedule of reinforcers would look like this:

+ + + + + | + | | | + | | | | | | | + | | | | | | | | | | +

Continuous ——————————————————— Intermittent
Fast Learning ————————————— Long Remembering

Now let us see how well we have explained when to use a continuous and when to use an intermittent schedule of reinforcers.

When Jane is learning a new process in mathematics, you should reinforce her correct solutions:

a. Every time

..................................Turn to page 28 (a).

b. Every other time

..................................Turn to page 28 (b).

c. At intermittent intervals

..................................Turn to page 28 (c).

a. You said you should reinforce her correct solutions every time.

You bet you should! A regular schedule of reinforcers makes for fast learning. Keep on selecting the right answers to our question and you will know the satisfaction Jane feels. Besides, you are positively reinforcing us as a writer of programs. Now turn to page 29.

b. You said we should reinforce her every other time.

Not unless we are "teaching" only half of the time. We want her to learn rapidly. Go back to the question on page 27 and select an answer that will continually convince her she is really on the right track.

c. You said we should reinforce her at intermittent intervals.

After she has learned the process this is a good idea. While she is beginning to learn, it will slow her down because she will not be sure she is right. Go back to the question on page 27 and choose an answer that will let her know every time she is right.

Once Jane has learned the new mathematics process, you want to make sure she remembers it even when you are not there to tell her she is right. To develop resistance to forgetting you change to:

a. a regular schedule of reinforcers

................................Turn to page 30 (a).

b. an intermittent schedule of reinforcers

................................Turn to page 30 (b).

c. some schedule related to the particular situation

................................Turn to page 30 (c).

a. A regular schedule of reinforcers. . . You said you would change to a regular schedule of reinforcers.

That would be no change at all. If you know your learning theory, you have been using a regular schedule and reinforcing her every time she has made the correct response so she will learn rapidly. Turn back to the question on page 29 and choose an answer that will make her new skill resistant to forgetting.

b. You said you would change to an intermittent schedule.

You have been doing careful reading. Once a response has been learned, when it is followed by a reinforcer some times and not others you always have hope that the next time will be reinforced. Slot machines are built on the principle that if they pay off occasionally, people will keep putting money into them. Las Vegas exists on intermittent reinforcers. Once people get a pay-off from gambling, just an occasional pay-off will keep them playing. Now turn to page 31.

c. You said you would change to some schedule related to the particular situation.

We would hope your behavior would be relevant to the situation as it was described. Go back to the question on page 29, re-read the question and choose the answer that will make the response resistant to extinction (forgetting).

To summarize:

When a student is learning a new behavior it should be reinforced (usually with a message of student's effort, competence and worth) every time: a continuous schedule.

Once the new behavior becomes reasonably predictable, the reinforcers should be spaced farther and farther apart — an intermittent schedule. Finally, just an occasional reinforcer will maintain that behavior and eventually no reinforcers will be needed. The student is productively in charge of self and feelings of worth and competence become internal reinforcers.

Spontaneous Recovery

One small matter remains to thwart us. We may have Sally's whining problem or Bill's tornado behavior all nicely solved and then after Christmas vacation we find, to our horror, that they have returned to their old behaviors which we have not seen since the middle of November. Spontaneous recovery is the term used to describe this reoccurrence of behavior you thought had been extinguished. It simply means that after a period of no appearance an old habit may ''recover'' enough once more to emerge. Again, it needs to be ''laid to rest'' by withholding reinforcement (ignoring the behavior). The temptation to ''blow your top'' must be sternly controlled so there is no reinforcement whatsoever, either positive or negative, and the old response can be extinguished. We will describe this process in the next chapter.

CHAPTER V
EXTINCTION OF INAPPROPRIATE BEHAVIORS

What about students who don't exhibit productive behaviors? We may feel we have nothing to reinforce. If we look carefully, however, we can usually change that "nothing" to "something" which may be "very little" or not as much as we would desire, but we can use any appropriate student behavior as a start for encouraging increased productive behavior. When we are annoyed by non-productive behaviors, it's easy to overlook productive behaviors in that student. (S)he may be in class on time, have materials ready, open the book to the correct page and audibly groan as we give the assignment. We always hear the groan but tend to ignore the preceeding productive behaviors. By accentuating the positive, "You got ready so quickly, you'll be finished in no time," we have reinforced the productive behaviors and have not reinforced the groan.

The very fact that we heard the groan should have alerted us that the student's purpose in emitting the sound was to get a reaction from us. Had we reacted, the student would have created the effect desired and "groaning" over assignments would have been reinforced. Resist the temptation to deliver a lecture on the importance of the assignment, how it will assist the student in later life, how rude it is to groan, etc. etc. etc. The student has dangled "bait" and if we take it, we're showing the intelligence of a fish.

If a student poked something and it wiggled, the student would poke it again. Students poke us to see if we will "wiggle". If we do, we have reinforced the poking. This illustrates why we use another important principle of reinforcement theory: *extinction.*

Extinction

Extinction (of the response, not the student!) means *no* reinforcer whatsoever. "Pay it no mind and it may go away," is good advice. Behaviors which are not reinforced drop out. "But should they get away with that behavior?" you ask. They are not "getting away with it" if the behavior doesn't get the response they wanted.

Answer this question, "Are teachers paid for punishing students who do 'wrong' or for teaching students to do 'right'?" If ignoring an inappropriate response is the most effective way to stop a student from making it, isn't that effective teaching?

An illustration from a graduate university class will make this point very clear. When learning about reinforcement, a high school English teacher asked, "If I have a student who cuts my class, doesn't turn in homework, and doesn't pay attention when he does come to class, doesn't he deserve an 'F'? Hasn't he earned an 'F'? Shouldn't I give him an 'F'?"

The professor responded, "Let's change that example. Suppose that same student went to a party and saw someone empty a bottle of vodka into the punch. The student knows that punch is 'spiked.' He knows he shouldn't drink alcohol but he has never tasted vodka and he is curious so he tries some. The punch is sweet and he can't taste the vodka, so he drinks more and more until his vision blurs and his movement is unsteady. He realizes he'd better get home and as he weaves out the door he misjudges distance, hits his shoulder on the door frame and almost falls. He knows his vision and movement are not functioning well, but he gets in his car, drives off, misses a sharp turn, goes over an embankment, smashes the car into a tree, and is badly injured. A doctor comes along. Shouldn't he let the student die? The student knew he shouldn't drink, that he was not fit to drive. Isn't dying what he has 'learned', what he 'deserves'? Why doesn't the doctor drive on and let him die? Because the doctor's job is to save that student if he possibly can, not to give him his just desserts. Our job as teachers is to save the student if we possibly can. Neither we nor the doctor can save all of them but we must try."

The hallmark of a professional is to deliver the service which is most enabling to the client. Not responding when a student "pokes" often constitutes that service. Ignoring actions which are a bid for attention usually is the fastest way of eliminating those behaviors. Obviously, we cannot ignore behavior which is a danger to others or to that student.

When a student makes a smart remark, one of the fastest ways to eliminate that behavior is to act as if you hadn't heard it and go right on teaching. "But what," you ask, "do you do when other students reinforce smart remarks by laughing, or when it is profane and you can't ignore it?"

You will be surprised that your ignoring the remark frequently becomes the model for other students and they, too, will ignore it. If they don't, or the remark is one that you can't ignore, a brief, "We won't take class time for that now, I'll see you at the end of the period," will accomplish three things: (1) the class knows there are going to be consequences but they don't know what they are, and the unknown is usually more feared than the known, (2) the "sinner" knows there are going to be consequences and it gives him/her the rest of the period to repent those sins and behave like a civilized student. Usually, a student will not add to the problem, knowing the time of reckoning is approaching. Then you can start with the positive, "When you made that silly remark, I wondered if you knew what was appropriate, but you were just great the rest of the period. Can I depend on that or do I need to do something?" Most students will say, "It's OK, I can handle it." "OK," you respond, "I'll watch and see if you do," and (3) it gives you time to determine appropriate consequences (and also calm down if necessary).

When you follow this procedure (1) the class knows something will happen, (2) the sinner knows something is going to happen and, most importantly, (3) it gives you time to figure out what *should* happen. Ad-hoc discipline, responding on the "spur of the moment," makes you reactive to student behaviors when you should be proactive on them. It never hurts to wait to discuss a problem: to say, "Mary, you are so frequently late for class, I'm going to think what might help. You think, too, and we'll decide what to do on Thursday." Often, this may be all that is needed to get Mary to class on time and then you have something to reinforce on Thursday.

Ignoring the blurted out response, then calling on a student who has raised a hand and responding with, "That's an excellent answer, you're really thinking," extinguishes the blurted out response and has the potential of making the "blurter-outer" wish (s)he had raised a hand and been recognized for a good idea. The science and the art of teaching is to immediately recognize that same blurting student when (s)he does raise a hand, "Great, Mary, your hand is up — let's hear your good idea." This action will go a long way in convincing the student there is virtue in hand raising.

When there is an annoying and persistent behavior, that behavior usually has been reinforced in the past or it wouldn't be so strong. Consequently, when we ignore a response that has worked in the past, students may try harder with the same response before they abandon it. When this increase of the undesirable behavior occurs right after we ignore it, although it can be discouraging to us, we know extinction is working even though it seems not to be. The "smart aleck" tries another louder remark. The interrupter interrupts louder. It takes will power, but we need to continue to ignore the increased irritant to convince the student the old behavior is no longer working. So, when you try extinction, expect that a response may increase before it dies out. When the light switch doesn't work, we flick it harder before we look for a different way to turn on the light. Students do the same.

"Pay it no mind," is an effective first response to undesirable behavior. (We are assuming there is not a safety factor involved. Students' safety cannot be ignored.) Should the undesirable behaviors not extinguish, however, a different strategy is indicated.

Productive behaviors can be encouraged or elicited by the use of positive reinforcers for most students. Non-productive behaviors are eliminated by extinction (Remember, you don't have to do this the rest of their lives). By the teacher's use of these techniques, students usually find productive behavior more satisfying and therefore preferable so they will elect to use them in the future as do all "self disciplined" people.

For those "free will zealots" who consider such techniques manipulative affronts to a student's free will, remember that the increase in behavioral productivity results in a gain for the student and only incidentally for the teacher. In the same way the physician's prescription results in a productive health gain for the patient and, incidentally, the satisfaction of successful practice for the doctor. When one person helps another achieve a goal, there always is satisfaction to both if the helper has "helping the person to no longer need help" as an outcome rather than the feeling of power over another.

Now, let us return to Bill and his problem of learning to enter the classroom as a student rather than a tornado. The teacher's "SOMETHING" (may have) suppressed the behavior that brought it on but when Bill tried different behavior, coming in quietly, nothing happened. Consequently, the new behavior was extinguished so he returned to his old habits. At first, the teacher needs to positively reinforce his new behavior ("Bill, you really know how a sixth grader takes care of himself") so that the likelihood of his continuing the new behavior will be increased.

Many responses are extinguished by withholding reinforcers. Stated as a common sense axiom, we don't keep on doing something that doesn't work. Sally has learned to fuss to get her way. If the teacher ignores it, eventually she will stop fussing to get her way with that particular teacher. This is assuming the behavior is not reinforced in some other way such as another adult or her playmates paying attention to her, or everyone else except her teacher giving in to the fussing. In that case it will take longer for the behavior to extinguish for that particular teacher, but eventually it will.

Scolding or ridicule may cause Sally to suppress the fussing but it will not cause the behavior to disappear. Sally has to learn there is no point in fussing because it doesn't get any results. To extinguish a response, nothing must happen as a result of it, i.e., it must have no reinforcement.

Let's look at a common example. Four-year-old Mike has just come out with his first (to our knowledge) "damn." While playing with a group in the sand box building project he said, "The damn truck won't work." Obviously, we would like to extinguish that part of his vocabulary. What should we do?

a. Be sure that he sees you looking horrified but say nothing

. . . . .Turn to page 38 (a).

b. Take him to one side and explain that this is not appropriate language

. . . . .Turn to page 38 (b).

c. Stop the play and give a responding lecture on swearing

. . . . .Turn to page 38 (c).

d. Act as if you had not heard it

. . . . .Turn to page 38 (d).

a. You said to be sure that he sees you looking horrified, but say nothing.

Horrifying a teacher is one of the most fun things a little boy can do. If he can get you to react like that to such a simple situation, who knows to what vocabulary heights he might ascend if he really put his mind to it? Besides, as a result of his language, nothing has happened to him — just to you. We also run the risk that he thinks we are horrified with him, not his behavior. The obvious conclusion is that we don't like him and that is not a nice feeling for any little boy. Go back to the question on page 37 and choose an answer that may extinguish his "damn."

b. You said to take him to one side and explain this is not appropriate language.

At least you have the sensitivity not to humiliate him in front of the group. Also, some members of the group might not have heard him and you are avoiding the undesirable possibility of teaching the word to those who may not know it. Nevertheless, if this is the first time the word has appeared, you are making too much of it. By so doing you are insuring that he will remember the word. Go back to the question on page 37 and choose an answer that has greater possibility of making him forget it.

c. You said to stop the play and give a resounding lecture on swearing.

You will accomplish one thing for sure. Everyone in the group (whether they knew it previously or not) will learn the word "damn." They will also learn it has the power of stopping whatever is going on and putting the teacher in orbit. Do not be surprised (if you have an alert group) that you will hear "damn" again from several sources. You had better go back to the question on page 37 and choose an answer that will have the opposite effect.

d. You said to act as if you had not heard it.

You are a rapid learner and a good reader because you noticed this was the *first* time this behavior had happened. When it produces no perceivable effect it is apt to be dropped. Remember, a response is extinguished by withholding the reinforcers. We usually do not continue to do things that produce no results.

No one can guarantee that he won't say "damn" again. Maybe he will get a response from his playmates or he has already "gotten" it from mother or dad. In spite of this, you have chosen the most appropriate action for the *first* time you have heard it. *Ignoring a response helps a student forget it.*

If he does not forget it, you will need to take a different action.

Now, turn to the next page.

CHAPTER VI
NEGATIVE REINFORCEMENT AND PUNISHMENT

No strategy is effective with every student, particularly if the undesirable behavior has worked (been reinforced) for several years, so let's look at what we can do with persistent, undesirable behaviors that don't respond to extinction. No behavior is permanent. As long as we're alive, our behavior can change. When positive reinforcers or extinction hasn't worked we may need to use negative reinforcers or punishment.

It seems to be a trait of humans, teachers included, that we look for "what's wrong" rather than "what's right." As a result, we often skip the power of positive reinforcement or extinction and move directly to negative reinforcement and punishment. In fact, when we ignore what a student is doing correctly, we may, unintentionally, be extinguishing productive behavior.

It should be with great care that we decide to deliberately beam a negative message to a student. It should be a *reflective* not *reflexive* act on our part. When, however, positive reinforcers and extinction aren't effective we turn to negative reinforcers to help students become more productively in charge of themselves.

Negative reinforcers

Humans will change their behaviors to eliminate or avoid unpleasant situations. If something unpleasant (negative reinforcer) is occurring and something the student does removes that unpleasant situation, the behavior that removed it is reinforced (strengthened) and is more likely to reoccur. We use this principle of negative reinforcement to make "reforming" on the part of the student work out well for him/her. If not having work done makes a student ineligible for some desired sport or club, and getting the work done results in inclusion in the desired activity, finishing work is strengthened (negatively reinforced) because it removes the undesirable situation of ineligibility and produces the desired situation.

Remember, reinforce means "to strengthen." We reinforce a behavior to increase the probability or frequency of that behavior. We cannot guarantee that the reinforced behavior will *always* be selected, but if reinforcement has occurred, the reinforced behavior will occur with higher probability than it did in the past.

Positive reinforcement (strengthening) results from the *addition* of something satisfying when a productive behavior occurs. Negative reinforcement (strengthening) results from the *subtraction* of something unpleasant or not satisfying. The *removal* of something unpleasant (aversive stimulus) has reinforced (strengthened) the behavior which immediately preceeded it.

Negative (-) reinforcement means that something undesirable has been subtracted or taken away. Removal, subtraction (-), rather than addition (+), has reinforced (strengthened) the behavior which the removal of something undesired immediately followed.

For example, you get in your car and start the motor with an unfastened seat belt. An unpleasant buzzing occurs. You fasten the belt. The buzzing stops. Fastening the belt has been negatively reinforced (strengthened) because it removed (subtracted) an unpleasant noise. Note that the buzzing and unproductive behavior (not fastening seat belt) were occurring simultaneously. A *change* of behavior (fastening the seat belt) cut off (subtracted) the buzzing and the new behavior (fastening the seat belt) was strengthened (negatively reinforced). The negative reinforcer was the removal of the buzzing sound.

All reinforcers are defined by their consequences. Positive reinforcement means strengthening of the behavior that brought on the positive reinforcer. Asking "please" brought on (added) the desired permission and the response became more probable. Negative reinforcement means strengthening of the behavior that removed (subtracted) the undesired buzzing (aversive stimulus) and fastening the belt became more probable. Note that car manufacturers, not understanding reinforcement theory, have made the noise pleasant (chimes) and have turned off the noise automatically after a short period, thereby reinforcing a person's ignoring the noise or "waiting it out" which removes the noise. As a result, for many people, both of those behaviors have become more probable than fastening the belt.

Negative reinforcement could be diagrammed as follows:
Example 1:

Not fastening seat belt _____ Behavior changed to fastening

Buzzing _____ Buzzing stopped
(Aversive stimulus) (Removed aversive stimulus) Fastening seat belt became stronger

Not fastening the seat belt and the buzzing occurred simultaneously. Because fastening the seat belt removed (cut off) the buzzing, that behavior became stronger (was negatively reinforced).

Example 2:

Not fastening seat belt and waiting _____ Waiting becomes stronger
because
Buzzing _____ (Automatically stopped)

Because the buzzer stopped while the driver was doing nothing but waiting, "waiting it out" was strengthened, because it got rid of (removed) the noise.

To use an analogy, a bridge can be strengthened by adding (+) something desirable (steel or girders) or it can be kept from collapsing by removing (-) all heavy tracks. In both cases the probability of the bridge remaining erect has been strengthened.

Let's look at a classroom example. Two girls are giggling and whispering. The teacher stops teaching and glares at the girls. The behaviors of girls giggling and teacher glaring are occurring simultaneously. The girls stop giggling and start listening (new behavior) which removes (subtracts) the teacher's glare, so listening is strengthened. Remember that reinforcers are defined by their results. If the listening behavior does not become more probable, negative reinforcement has not occurred regardless of how much glaring the teacher does.

Negative reinforcement is important to self discipline because *the student is in charge of what happens.* When the person changes behavior (fastening seat belts, stopping giggling), (s)he can remove the negative reinforcers. Negative reinforcement also can be dangerous because any behavior which removes the undesired (aversive stimulus), disconnecting buzzer, pretending to pay attention, lying, cheating, blaming others will be strengthened.

Punishment

Punishment is the addition (+) of undesirable consequences in an attempt to suppress a behavior. You get a ticket (punishment) if you drive without a fastened seat belt. The teacher may say to the giggly girls, "You will stay after school." In the case of punishment, the person is not able to remove this unpleasant consequence by changing behavior at this point. Only the police officer or the teacher can remove those consequences.

But, here is where negative reinforcement and punishment become fuzzy concepts. In the future, the *memory* of the threat of punishment can become an internal negative reinforcer. To remove the possibility of getting a ticket, the motorist may fasten the belt and experience the negative reinforcer of relief from worry about a ticket. The girls may want to giggle and talk, but they can remove the unpleasant possibility of staying after school by looking attentive and listening to the teacher, so those behaviors have been negatively reinforced (strengthened). Now, if the teacher understands reinforcement theory, (s)he will add a positive reinforcer to the listening behavior. ''Many of you (looking right at the girls) are listening so carefully, you will know this so well you won't have to study for the test,'' thereby increasing, through an anonymous positive reinforcer, the probability of listening behavior in the future.

If, in spite of the author's efforts, the distinctions between negative reinforcement and punishment are not completely clear, don't worry about it. Lots of people who don't understand electricity use it very effectively. The author has watched many teachers use reinforcement theory so it was a symphony of translating theory into artistic performance. Those teachers' explanations of what they were doing might be incorrect or a garbled mess which no one could understand. Conversely, some psychologists can articulate theory with precision, but don't use it effectively to increase productive learning in their own university classes.

So, if you can't clearly describe the difference between negative reinforcement and punishment, don't worry. Just use both with artistry and with dignity to your students, so they become increasingly in charge and responsible for their own behavior. Just ask yourself the question, ''By changing behavior, could the student remove the unpleasant situation?'' That will tell you whether the student is having the opportunity to be in charge of self. Then you have accomplished the objective of a professional. The client may no longer need you.

We may need to clarify in more detail the difference between negative reinforcement, punishment, and extinction. Punishment helps a student know what not to do. If Jane hits another student to get a turn and the teacher benches her (punishment) she knows she should not hit. The benching may suppress the hitting, but she still has not practiced an appropriate way to get the turn.

If the teacher says, ''Remember, if you hit, you'll be benched, if you stand in line you'll get a turn.'' The student knows what to do. By standing in line, Jane has removed being benched (negative reinforcer) and she gets a turn which is what she wants.

If Jane hits another student to get a turn and the other student ignores her, that is, the other student does nothing back to Jane but does not give up the turn, Jane learns that hitting does not secure the turn. Nothing has happened as a result of the hitting, so she probably will try some other way of getting a turn. The hitting response has been extinguished because it was not reinforced. Now, if by hitting, Jane gets another student to give up a turn, the hitting has been positively reinforced and Jane will hit again.

Let us see how clear we have made this. Bob is a bully and he threatens other children with physical harm if they do not let him be pitcher in the ball game. The children are afraid of him and let him have his way. His behavior of threatening has been:

a. Positively reinforced

. . . . .Turn to page 44 (a).

b. Negatively reinforced

. . . . .Turn to page 44 (b).

c. Extinguished

. . . . .Turn to page 44 (c).

a. You said that his threatening behavior had been positively reinforced.

I'll say it has! It works so well that it will probably reoccur whenever he wants to be pitcher or anything else. You understand the principle of positive reinforcement.

Now turn to page 45.

b. You said his threatening behavior has been negatively reinforced.

Unfortunately not! We wish it had been. His being a bully worked so well he will try it again. Turn back to the question on page 43 and select an answer that shows his response of threatening will probably happen again when he wants to be pitcher.

c. You said his threatening behavior has been extinguished.

We wish it had been, but this only happens when threatening gets him no place. His threat got him the pitcher's spot. Turn back to the question on page 43 and choose an answer that will explain why he will probably act the same obnoxious way next time.

Let us suppose that this time Bob threatens other students and as a result the teacher puts him out of the game. His threatening has been:

a. Positively reinforced

. . . . Turn to page 46 (a).

b. Punished

. . . . Turn to page 46 (b).

c. Extinguished

. . . . Turn to page 46 (c).

a. You said Bob's threatening behavior had been positively reinforced.

Thank goodness it was not! If it had been positively reinforced he would get the pitching job and threatening would be likely to happen again. The teacher put him out of the game so he would *not* be so likely to act that way again. Turn back to the question on page 45 and choose an answer that shows his threatening response has been suppressed.

b. You said that Bob's threatening behavior had been punished.

Right you are! Being put out of the game is something he does not like, so even though he wants to threaten other children, he will refrain from doing it, because if he doesn't, he won't get to play at all. The punishment (putting him out of the game) has suppressed his threatening response but he still has not practiced what he *should* do to get to be pitcher.

Turn to page 47.

c. You said his threatening response has been extinguished.

Unfortunately not. When the teacher is not there to put him out of the game he will probably go back to his old bullying ways. Go back to the question on page 45 and choose an answer that shows his threatening has only been suppressed by the action of the teacher.

Now let us suppose that Bob begins to play with other students who are too big to be scared of him. Every time he threatens to hurt them if they do not let him pitch, they just ignore him and go on with the game. If he tries to hit one of the bigger boys, he is simply brushed off. His threatening is getting him nowhere so it is being:

a. Positively reinforced

. . . . Turn to page 48 (top).

b. Negatively reinforced

. . . . Turn to page 48 (middle).

c. Extinguished

. . . . Turn to page 48 (bottom).

a. You said his threatening behavior was positively reinforced.

Thank goodness it was not. It didn't get him the pitching position; it got him ignored. Go back to the question on page 47 and choose an answer that shows his threatening is getting neither good not bad results.

b. You said his threatening was negatively reinforced.

It could not have been, because nothing unpleasant was removed. He was just ignored. Go back to the question on page 47 and choose an answer that shows there was no reinforcement of any kind.

c. You said his threatening behavior was extinguished.

Right you are! Nothing was happening as a result of his threatening so there was little point in trying it again. The absence of any kind of reinforcer will probably extinguish the behavior.

Now turn to page 49.

Let us look at an example of application of all three of these principles (positive reinforcement, negative reinforcement, and extinguishing a response) as they might apply to whining Sally. For obvious reasons we are simplifying behavior to identify principles, and this in no way should be taken as a what-to-do-about-whining recipe.

Sally has learned to whine to get her way. Obviously, this has worked (been positively reinforced) in the past or she would not continue to do it. Knowing this keeps us from the error of expecting a rapid, overnight miracle to occur or hoping that by just ignoring whining it will go away (be extinguished). We need to change her behavior and place her in charge of selecting more appropriate ways to achieve what she wants. Our number one task is determining a new, more appropriate behavior so she can express her desires. There's nothing wrong with expressing preferences, Sally has simply learned an inappropriate way to do it. Too often we terminate our thinking at the ''stop whining'' point without proceeding to the ''start. . . '' level. Do we want her to learn to say, ''Please, may I. . . ?'' Do we want her to learn to flatter people to get her way? Do we want her to hit someone so they will give in? You recoil in horror, yet these all could be more effective than whining to get one's way.

Thinking the problem through, you will probably come to the conclusion that the behavior you want to teach is two-fold: (1) learning socially acceptable ways of persuasion (politeness, making the other person feel comfortable); (2) learning socially acceptable ways of dealing with your disappointment when you are not successful (going along with the majority, being a good sport).

In this analysis of behavior lies the tremendous dividends from the application of theory into practice. No longer will you be fuzzy in your thinking, for you must *identify the specific behavior you wish to change and then define with exactness the new behavior the child is to learn*. Otherwise, you have no idea what it is you are going to teach the student to do and positively reinforce when it occurs.

In Sally's case, we want to suppress the whining behavior so she will have a chance to learn to say, ''Please, may I,'' and be a good sport if that does not work.

We start by identifying with her the specific behavior to be changed, letting her know that whining is not acceptable, then help her practice ways of expressing her desires appropriately. Skillfully stimulated and guided by us, this identification can come out of her (''What did you do when you wanted the ball? Did you get it? Can you think of a way that might have worked? Has this happened to other people? What did they do? Did that seem to work?'') *This step of identification of the unacceptable behavior and the replacement behavior with the student is essential for efficient and economical use of time and energy.* There is no point in trying to sneak up on a problem or hope that a learner can guess whether it is the whining or wanting to be first that is unacceptable.

If the undesirable behavior is long standing, it may be necessary to change it by negative reinforcers or suppress it by punishment so another behavior can be learned in its place (''If you whine, you will have to leave the game and sit on the bench''). The minute the desired behavior is emitted it needs to be heavily reinforced (''Good for you, Sally, you're being such a good sport, you get the ball next''). Remember, the new behavior has to work for the student or it will be extinguished.

As soon as the desired behavior (being a good sport) has been identified and reinforced enough times so it is more likely to occur than the previous whining behavior, we remove the negative reinforcer (benching) from the undesirable behavior. Then we can extinguish it by allowing it to come out unreinforced (no one pays attention to her whining) while continuing to positively reinforce the desirable behavior, at first on a continuous and then on an intermittent schedule.

Psychological jargon translated into Sally's behavior means that as soon as she has learned to sometimes say ''please'' and to be a good sport, we stop benching her, but ignore her whining. If it is appropriate, we praise or reward her for being a good sport. When she whines we must ignore her (and insist that others do the same). The whining should drop out of her repertoire of responses (be extinguished) while politeness and sportsmanship will become more and more likely to reoccur as a result of their being reinforced.

You may not be sure of when to negatively reinforce and when to ignore (extinguish by withholding reinforcement). It will help to estimate how often the undesirable response has occurred. If it is a new response or has not happened many times, you can ignore it. Not getting results (no reinforcement) will probably cause the student to abandon that behavior (extinction).

If the undesirable response has happened many times, you can be sure it has worked (been positively reinforced) or the student would not continue to use it. Therefore, the undesirable response may need to be changed by negative reinforcement or suppressed by punishment until some desirable response has a chance to become strong enough (as a result of positive or negative reinforcement) to take the place of the undesirable one, i.e., be more likely to occur.

It may help if we put these ideas in another context. With a student who is having problems, it is as if you had a strong runner (undesirable behavior) and a weak runner (desirable behavior) racing for a prize. The strong runner is used to winning so you hold him back (punishment or negative reinforcement), and let the weak runner win the race and get the prize (positive reinforcement). You keep on doing this until the weak runner has had so much practice his legs are getting very strong and he enjoys running for the prize. When you think he has practiced enough that he can beat the strong runner, you "let go" of the formerly strong runner you have been holding back (remove the punishment or negative reinforcement) so they can both race. As the previously weak runner (desirable behavior) keeps on winning (positive reinforcement), the formerly strong runner (undesirable behavior) gives up (is extinguished) because he never wins anything (no reinforcement). He won't give up as long as he is held back, but if he keeps on losing (no reinforcement), he will.

Once Jane, who is apprehensive about math, has learned the new mathematics process, you want to make sure she remembers it even when you are not there to tell her she is right. To develop resistance to forgetting, you change to:

a. a regular schedule of reinforcers

. . . . .Turn to page 54 (a).

b. an intermittent schedule of reinforcers

. . . . .Turn to page 54 (b).

c. some schedule related to the particular situation

. . . . .Turn to page 54 (c).

a. You said you would change to a regular schedule of reinforcers.

That would be no change at all. If you know your learning theory, you have been using a regular schedule and reinforcing her every time she has made the correct response so she will learn rapidly. Turn back to the question on page 53 and choose an answer that will make her new skill resistant to forgetting.

b. You said you would change to an intermittent schedule.

You have been doing careful reading. Once a response has been learned, when it is followed by a reinforcer some times and not others, there is always hope that the next time will be reinforced. Slot machines are built on the principle that if they pay off occasionally, people will keep putting money into them. Las Vegas exists on intermittent reinforcers. Once people get a payoff from gambling, just an occasional pay-off will keep them playing.

Turn now to page 55.

c. You said you would change to some schedule related to the particular situation.

We would hope your behavior would be relevant to the situation as it was described. Go back to the question on page 53, re-read the question, and choose the answer that will make the response resistant to extinction (forgetting).

When a student is learning a new behavior, it should be reinforced (usually with a message of effort, competence, and worth) every time — a continuous schedule.

Once the new behavior becomes reasonably predictable, the reinforcers should be spaced farther and farther apart — an intermittent schedule. Finally, just an occasional reinforcer will maintain that behavior and eventually no reinforcers will be needed. The student has become productively in charge of self and the feelings of worth and competence become internal reinforcers.

You have read about the four most important concepts of reinforcement — positive, negative, extinction, and schedule. Why then can't we shape behavior as easily and successfully in the classroom as we can in a psychology laboratory? Here again theory helps us understand. By the time the student arrives at our classroom door (s)he has a long history of conditioning and reinforcement. How many thousand times has a student interrupted, whined, fought, or been a poor sport before someone decided to do something about it? As we said before, it must have worked or (s)he would not be continuing it. The behavior would have been extinguished.

The problem is compounded by the fact that, in most cases, other people have attempted to change the undesirable behavior and have given up. (Sally's mother decides she is not going to give in to whining so she resists it a few times and then capitulates.) As a result, the behavior has received reinforcement on an intermittent schedule which makes it more resistant to extinction.

To summarize:

Reinforcement means "strengthening" a behavior — making it more probable or more frequent.

Positive reinforcement means "strengthening" a behavior by *addition* of something needed or desired immediately after the behavior occurs. The *addition* of something desirable acts as a reinforcer.

Negative reinforcement means "strengthening" a behavior by *subtraction* of something undesirable immediately after that behavior has occurred. The *removal* of something undesirable acts as a reinforcer.

Punishment means the *addition* of an undesirable consequence in order to suppress a behavior. The memory or threat of a punishment can become a negative reinforcer.

.

When John makes a smart remark in class and you ignore it, and go right on with the lesson it means you:

a. Think it's just a bad habit of his

. . . . Turn to page 58 (a).

b. Think it is a relatively new response for him

. . . . Turn to page 58 (b).

c. Are not sure what you should do

. . . . Turn to page 58 (c).

a. You said you thought it was a bad habit.

If a response is habitual, it must be getting some results, so your ignoring it would be useless. You will have to suppress it by punishment or use negative reinforcers so he can learn a more productive response in its place. Go back to page 57 and select an answer that indicates you think ignoring the behavior will take care of the problem.

b. You said you thought it was a relatively new response for him.

Then you did just the right thing! If it were new behavior, John was probably trying it out to see what would happen. When he sees it produces no results, either positive or negative, he probably will eventually abandon it (he may try it again to be sure it won't work). In addition, your ignoring it will set a behavior model for the rest of the class. If smart remarks do not get a big reaction from you, there will be little point in trying them.

Turn to page 59.

c. You said you were not sure what you should do.

As a teacher this is not the first nor last time you will find yourself in this fix. However, you have just created an aversive stimulus for the writer of this program for not writing more clearly, so turn back to page 57 and re-read the material there. Also you have caused us to change our ways so writing more clearly will be reinforced.

Now let us assume that you ignore John's smart (and rude) remark but he continues to make them and it puts the rest of the class in hysterics. At this point you should decide to:

a. Keep on ignoring the behavior
. . . . Turn to page 60 (a).

b. Negatively reinforce or punish John
. . . . Turn to page 60 (b).

c. Negatively reinforce the class
. . . . Turn to page 60 (c).

a. You said you would keep on ignoring the behavior.

If you do, you have more ability to tolerate misbehavior than most teachers. You will need it too, as the class sees someone can continue to get by with unacceptable classroom manners. Remember, this is not the first time, in which case you would have tried extinction.

Turn back to the question on page 59 and select an answer that will give a boy assistance in developing the self control he lacks.

b. You said you would need to negatively reinforce or punish John.

Right! John needs some help in controlling himself. For his sake, and yours, that kind of behavior should be suppressed. Whether you use a negative reinforcer or punishment depends on John's personality. Whether you quietly say, "Let's plan a time when we can talk after class," or you suspend him from your class depends on your judgment of which is more appropriate. The wiser your decision the more effective will be the outcome. Remember that the behavior that removes your negative reinforcer will be strengthened so you had better be sure that it is desirable behavior.

Now turn to page 61.

c. You said you would negatively reinforce or punish the class.

You would, no doubt, feel like it but John is the culprit with whom you begin. The class may be looking to you to control John and then they will control themselves. Later, you may need to work with the class so they don't respond (extinguish) John's response. Turn back to the question on page 59 and choose an answer that will assist John in suppressing his rudeness and learning better ways of participating.

An important aspect of our understanding of reinforcement is that while we usually associate praise and reward with positive reinforcement and punishment with negative reinforcement, this is not necessarily so. Shy Tommy might find public praise a very embarrassing and undesirable negative reinforcer, and attention-seeking Paul might find a public scolding very rewarding to his needs (positive reinforcement). As a result, while we can make some general assumptions, it is always necessary to correct them by an estimate of what constitutes reward and punishment for a particular student. "Identifying the reward system to which (s)he responds" is the way we say it psychologically.

The last important consideration to which we must attend, is that emotions and attitudes are responses which students may not control; but they become associated with the actions that bring rewards and punishment. As a result, these emotions and attitudes are conditioned in a respondent fashion like Pavlov's salivating dog. We don't need to worry about our positive reinforcers, but we need to be concerned about the environment and emotions that may become conditioned by punishment or loss of dignity. It is this aspect that makes punishment a dangerous weapon.

A student who loses dignity usually becomes rebellious and resistant in the situation and retaliatory to the person who caused the loss of dignity. Scolding or benching Sally may suppress her whining, but it may also teach her that teachers are mean, games are not fun, and the play yard is a place to be avoided by playing in the girls' lavatory. Being punished or losing dignity can become associated with teacher, subject, or school, an emotion that will interfere with future learning.

Knowing reinforcement theory makes you realize that corporal punishment is not a good idea because:

a. It is an old-fashioned punishment
. . . . .Turn to page 64 (a).

b. It is ineffective
. . . . .Turn to page 64 (b).

c. It is too hard on the teacher
. . . . .Turn to page 64 (c).

d. Undesirable emotions and attitudes are conditioned by it
. . . . .Turn to page 64 (d).

a. You said it is an old-fashioned punishment.

It is old-fashioned, but so are honesty and integrity. Being old-fashioned can be a virtue as well as something to be discarded. Go back to the question on page 63 and choose an answer that describes why corporal punishment is not desirable.

b. You said it is ineffective in most cases.

Usually it is. Nevertheless, a good spanking may stop an inappropriate or dangerous behavior. We agree that there are more effective ways to change that behavior. Go back to the question on page 63 and choose an answer that will more precisely describe the undesirable results of corporal punishment.

c. You said it is too hard on the teacher.

If you know anything harder than good teaching, we will put in with you. Granted, if you have ever spanked a student it is an extremely unpleasant memory; but if it would work, it might be worth it. Go back to the question on page 63 and choose an answer that will supply the reason for your not doing it.

d. You said undesirable emotions and attitudes are conditioned by corporal punishment.

They certainly are! A student may learn not to do a certain thing as a result of a spanking. He also will possibly learn to dislike school, that teachers are mean, rules are not fair, and to get even the first chance he has. All of these compounding factors make corporal punishment educationally unsound. There are many other undesirable consequences that are just as effective (or more so) and do not have undesirable side effects.

Now turn to page 65.

When a student has been playing during work time, most of us have tried the technique of telling him he may do his work now or after school (negative reinforcer, he is in charge of what will happen). He doesn't finish, so we keep him after school to finish his work (punishment). Which behavior do we wish to suppress by keeping him after school?

a. Not taking his work seriously

.... Turn to page 66 (a).

b. Playing during work time

.... Turn to page 66 (b).

c. Poor work habits

.... Turn to page 66 (c).

d. Not minding the teacher

.... Turn to page 66 (d).

a. You said we wanted to suppress his not taking his work seriously.

Of course, we would like him to think the work is meaningful and important but unfortunately not all school work is. If he were so serious he went over each problem five times, he probably would not finish and he would still need to stay after school. Go back to the question on page 65 and look for the *specific* behavior we want to suppress.

b. You said we wanted to suppress his playing during work time.

Right you are! And about time we did something about it. As long as he plays when he should be working, he will never be able to devote his full energies to the task at hand, so the sooner we suppress this behavior the better. This is not to say that playing isn't normal and to be expected but society (and his future boss) won't accept playing when he should be working.

Now turn to page 67.

c. You said we wanted to suppress his poor work habits.

He has poor work habits all right but this is a pervasive trait and our punishment will suppress a specific behavior. We cannot hope to redesign his whole outlook on life with such a specific punishment as keeping him after school. Go back to the question on page 65 and look for the specific behavior we want to suppress.

d. You said we wanted to suppress his not minding the teacher.

It sounds like a desirable goal but what if someone uses poor judgment in giving orders. Should he mind then without thinking? Besides, we don't know that the teacher said, "Now work and don't play." Maybe if you asked him what the teacher said, he would look at you blankly because he had not even thought about it — he was just enjoying himself. Go back to the question on page 65 and look for the *specific* behavior we want to suppress.

Now that we have established that the punishment of keeping a boy after school could suppress his playing during work time, what response are we strengthening? Negative reinforcement strengthens the response that takes away the negative reinforcer (staying after school). What will take away this negative reinforcer and thereby be the response that is strengthened?

a. Finishing his work
.....................................Turn to page 68 (a).

b. Paying attention
.....................................Turn to page 68 (b).

c. Taking his work seriously
.....................................Turn to page 68 (c).

d. Having his mother write a note that he is not to be kept after school
.....................................Turn to page 68 (d).

a. You said that the response of finishing his work would be strengthened.

Now you are thinking from theory! The minute he finishes, he's excused to go home and his staying after school is terminated. That is, unless his teacher feels compelled to give him a moral lecture. If (s)he does, (s)he has probably lost the ground gained by punishment. If (s)he compliments him and excuses him the minute he is finished, he should learn that by doing what he is supposed to do, he will have approval and not have to stay after school.

Turn to page 69.

b. You said his response of paying attention would be strengthened.

Don't we wish it! But it is not that easy. Suppose he listened as hard as he could but just did not get it. He would not be able to do the work and finish. Besides, if he is a whiz in math, he would not have to listen at all, and he could figure it out and get done in time. Maddening, isn't it? You had better turn back to the question on page 67 and choose an answer that is more likely to happen.

c. You said taking his work seriously would be strengthened.

Could be, but we cannot count on it. Plodding Paul, who works like a dog may not finish, but Flashy Freddy can whip it out in a few minutes. Think about what behavior took away staying after school. Turn back to the question on page 67 and make another choice.

d. You said the response of having his mother write a note that he is not to be kept after school would be strengthened.

Not if he is in my school and I hope not in yours! If you choose this you must have been pushed around by parents, so quickly turn back to the question on page 67 and make another choice.

Remember, negative reinforcement strengthens any response that takes away the negative reinforcer. Consequently, when cheating takes away poor grades, when day-dreaming takes away attending to work, when "telling a story" takes away consequences, all of these undesirable responses are being strengthened. This is one of the dangers of negative reinforcement. We must identify desirable behavior to replace the undesirable behavior. Then we must elicit the desirable behavior and consciously and systematically reinforce it. This is the only way we can be sure that some unproductive behavior (cheating, falsifying, withdrawing) which takes away the negative reinforcer is not inadvertently being reinforced.

We now have a boy who, by staying after school, had his behavior of playing during work time suppressed (we hope) and his behavior of finishing his work strengthened. In the future, finishing will take away the negative reinforcer of the possibility of staying after school. What can we do to increase further the probability that he will finish his work the next time that we give an assignment? (If he had been smart enough to throw up, we would have let him go home too, wouldn't we, but we don't want *that* to happen again.) Think about what you have learned to do to increase the probability of a response reoccurring.

To further strengthen "finishing work," we would:

a. Point out the importance of finishing work

.....................................Turn to page 72 (a).

b. Calculate the amount of playtime he has missed

.....................................Turn to page 72 (b).

c. Show him how much of our time he has taken

.....................................Turn to page 72 (c).

d. Compliment him for finishing his work

.....................................Turn to page 72 (d).

a. You said we would point out to him the importance of finishing his work.

How many thousand times do you think this has happened to a student who does not finish? Obviously, it was a useless technique or he wouldn't still be having the problem. He has probably learned long ago to turn off his hearing aid when adults start to lecture. Go back to page 71 and select an answer that he will be more likely to hear.

b. You said we should calculate the amount of playtime he has missed.

This might give him some arithmetic practice but we doubt it. Knowing the answer will probably confirm his suspicion that school takes too much time out of the more important aspects of the the day and he had better sandwich more play periods into the school schedule. Go back to the question on page 71 and select an answer that will increase his desire to work.

c. You said to show him how much of our time he has taken.

Depending on what kind of a fiend he is, he may shout for joy. After all, aren't we taking his time with our silly assignments? If he is truly sorry, all we have done is make him feel guilty which will in no way help him attend to his assignments. Go back to the question on page 71 and select an answer that will increase his desire to work.

d. You said we should compliment him for finishing his work.

Excellent! You have learned to use positive reinforcement to increase the probability of a response. If we say, "You worked hard and did a fine job, I had no idea you could do so well. I thought perhaps you were not finishing because the work was too hard," he is going to be more apt to finish his next paper and get some more praise. The tiny hint of negative reinforcement we added (the humiliation of not being able to do the work) should suppress "not finishing" and strengthen showing you he *can* do the work. Of course, we tailor what we say and do to the needs and maturity level of the child. The words we use with a five-year-old are insulting to a fourteen-year-old. The theory is the same, however. All of them (and we) respond favorably to anything that makes us feel adequate and appreciated. You are finding that this psychological theory is really very easy to understand, isn't it? You are ready to turn to the next page.

CHAPTER VII
THERAPEUTIC NEGATIVE REINFORCERS

When a behavior is strengthened (made more probable or frequent) by the removal of an aversive stimulus (something undesirable) which leaves the student in a more pleasant state, that strengthening is termed *negative reinforcement*. Negative reinforcers are useful because they leave the learner in charge. Negative reinforcers also can be dangerous and can lead to undesirable behaviors because *anything* that removes the aversive stimulus could be strengthened. Lying, stealing, cheating, blaming others, psychosomatizing all result from their success in removing something aversive. Consequently, when we are using negative reinforcers we need to be sure that only *desirable* behaviors remove them.

A "therapeutic" negative reinforcer is one that has high probability of being successful, but maintains students' dignity, something none of us can tolerate losing, and encourages them to develop self discipline.

The following are some negative reinforcers that have high probability of being successful and maintaining dignity.

Proximity

The closer we are to an authority figure, the more obedient we are. You know what you do when you see the police car in your rear view mirror. You "straighten up and drive right!" We know that when teachers are in the halls during passing times, students' behavior improves. When principals consistently make a "sweep" of the cafeteria or yard, behavior usually is better. The police patrol car has the same effect as it cruises through a neighborhood.

Knowing this, it is usually effective to go over to or stand by a student who is not behaving appropriately (talking, pushing, playing with something, not paying attention) while continuing to teach. The student knows why you are there and that you are doing it deliberately, but no one else knows it so there is no loss of dignity and the student is encouraged to direct him/herself to more acceptable behavior.

Obviously, this strategy eliminates dignity destroying discipline tactics such as calling across the room, "Bill, put that away!" or "Mary and Sue, stop that talking!" which can trigger undesirable, dignity restoring tactics such as "I need it to work," or "I wasn't talking!" which starts a verbal tug of war between student and teacher.

It's amazing how many discipline problems can be eliminated by proximity with no exchange of words. Students do not want a teacher near them when they are not behaving appropriately (We don't want a policeman near when we miss a boulevard stop). The teacher, in this case, becomes a negative reinforcer. As soon as the student is behaving appropriately, the teacher moves away. "Behaving appropriately" has removed the close presence of the teacher. Consequently, the appropriate behavior has been negatively reinforced; made stronger (When we drive appropriately, the policeman passes us and moves on).

Use of the Student's Name

It is impossible to ignore your name when you hear or see it. Consequently, one way of getting a misbehaving or inattentive student's attention is through use of that student's name in a *positive* way. In a lesson on descriptive language, "Suppose Mary," (who is talking to a neighbor) "earned money by baby sitting. She wanted to distribute some ads about her service. What are some adjectives she might use in her ad to make people want to hire her? Mary, you be the teacher and call on people who have their hands up." Mary finds she must participate in the lesson, but it is nonthreatening because she doesn't have to think of words and it is rewarding because she hears positive things about herself; "dependable," "honest," "careful," "safe." Mary usually knows why the teacher used her as an example. She realizes the teacher did it deliberately, however, there was no affront to her dignity, and when she stopped talking she heard good things about herself. Her stopping talking was negatively reinforced, it left her in a more pleasant state, therefore, not talking became more probable.

Some people ask, "Why should Mary hear good things about herself when she is misbehaving?" The answer is that you want to help her learn to behave. Remember, our job is to save them, not to give them what they deserve. Sometimes the above strategies won't work. *Nothing always works with the human.* It may be necessary to move Mary away from her friend. Again, this needs to be done with dignity. "We need someone to record these words. Mary, please come up to the board and be our secretary." Mary comes to the board and records. The teacher continues, "Mary, you are a good secretary. Sit right here so we can use you again when we need you." The teacher indicates a chair in the front of the room, away from her friend. Mary knows she's been moved. She knows the teacher did it on purpose, but no one else knows. There is no loss of dignity.

Signaling the Student

Frequently, a teacher can signal a student to change behavior with no use of words. A "look" accompanied by a gesture to the teacher's ear signals,

"You need to listen." A slight shake of the head signals, "You need to stop that." With a brush of the hand, a student is signaled, "Put that away." A touch to the mouth conveys, "Your mouth is out of order." A teacher's eyes become very powerful message conveyers. A teacher's "look" can give a student an important reminder with no other student being aware that an unmistakable message has been sent and received.

Sometimes a prearranged signal is agreed upon by student and teacher. This is particularly effective when a student has engaged in a behavior so often that (s)he is not aware it is occurring. Drumming, arguing, getting off the subject, day dreaming, playing with something, doodling can become so habitual that they are unnoticed by the student who is engaging in that behavior. A mutually agreed upon signal from the teacher will bring that behavior to a conscious level so the student is aware of and can terminate the undesirable behavior.

Private Reminders to the Student

Sometimes, there needs to be disciplinary verbal communication between teacher and student. To avoid loss of dignity, the class is given a short task, related to what is being taught in the lesson, to occupy their attention and give the teacher an opportunity to privately and unobtrusively cue the offending student. "Everyone write a sentence about yourself with a dependent clause (make up a problem, summarize our discussion). You'll have a minute to do it, then I'll call on some of you to read yours and we'll practice punctuating them." Students feel accountable for producing a product and the teacher has time to go to the offending student(s) and quietly say, "Bill and Tom, I've tried several times to signal you to stop talking. Can you take care of it or does one of you need to move?" Usually, they will say, "It's OK, Mrs. Hunter, we'll stop." To which the teacher responds, "I know you can if you choose to. Should you forget, let's decide, now, which one of you I will signal to move." That decided, the teacher continues with the class, "Do we have a volunteer to read a sentence?" or "Susie, read your sentence."

Note, the two boys are in charge of whether they are separated. If they want to sit together, the possibility of being separated is the negative reinforcer they can remove by not talking. Thus, they develop self discipline.

Recording Student Behavior

"It is in your record," is an ominous signal to any of us. Making a *private* (not one that can be read by the rest of the class!) record of the student's behavior will signal that it is not going unnoticed or without possible consequences, but there is no public humiliation. It is a negative reinforcer because the student can stop the recording as soon as (s)he ceases to engage in the behavior being recorded.

If you feel the student is doing something to get attention or "get your goat," you are wise to pretend you haven't seen or heard it. This has high probability of extinguishing the behavior. When you respond *in any way*, you have positively reinforced the undesired behavior because it got the student the response ("gotcha") (s)he wanted.

Obviously, you cannot ignore an unsafe behavior or one that infringes on the rights of others, but it's amazing how many "bids for attention" such as smart remarks or noises disappear when they don't get the desired results.

"What," you ask, "do you do when the rest of the class gives the student attention?" Often, if you ignore it, students soon will. If they don't, you might say, with or without the student's presence depending on which, in your best judgement, would be more productive "If Bill asked you how to spell a word and you deliberately taught him the incorrect spelling, you are doing something that will make him look foolish later. You are doing the same thing if you laugh at a silly remark. You are teaching him that is a good way to get attention and later it will make him look foolish to others. So if he says something silly and you laugh, you will be in trouble." To the "We can't help it" excuse, your response is, "Oh yes, you can. You are in charge of what you do." Take no excuses and the students will see you mean it. Of course, if his remark is really funny, laugh with them and go on with the business of teaching and learning.

You might, also, when a silly remark is made, pick up a pad and pencil and, in a moment of silence with no comment, record it. In rare cases, you might check the accuracy with the student, "Bill, did you say, 'all teachers are old and dumb' or 'dumb and old'?" This can elicit, "What are you going to do with that?" from the culprit. Your response can be, "I haven't decided yet." Remember, the unknown is often more feared than the known.

Usually, just the silence and recording with no comment are all that are necessary. "Won't the others notice?" you ask. Yes, but they don't know what you are writing and, remember, it is up to that student whether you do it again. (S)he can stop the recording (remove the negative reinforcer) any moment the behavior that triggered the recording ceases.

Sometimes you give prior *private* notice. "Susan, I don't think you realize how many times you call out the answer not giving others time to think. I'm going to record each time on this pad so at the end of the period you can see what a habit it is. Remember, if you raise your hand, I'll call on you." Every time she raises her hand, you need to call on her so she sees the appropriate behavior works. You won't have to keep doing it. You can vary by saying, "Susan, you be the teacher and call on someone," or "Susan knows. Let's wait for more hands."

The strategies of proximity, use of a name, signaling, private reminders, and recording will handle *almost* all discipline, but not all. Sometimes it is necessary to hold a private conference with the student away from the class. If outside of class time is not possible, take the student to the *back* of the room while the class is working on an independent assignment. Seat the student, back to the class, while you face the class, so if any curious student turns around to see what is going on, you can signal that student to get back to work.

Prepare as carefully for that conference as you would for any difficult lesson, for changing behavior is difficult *teaching*, not admonishing or giving orders. The next chapter on strategies for changing behavior will identify the critical steps in planning and conducting a conference when therapeutic negative reinforcers haven't worked.

CHAPTER VIII
DESIGNING AND CONDUCTING A
DISCIPLINARY CONFERENCE

A behavioral conference needs to be planned even more carefully than a difficult lesson because the student has already "failed" in the content to be learned. Learning to replace a response by a more appropriate one is more difficult than to have learned the appropriate one the first place.

PLANNING THE CONFERENCE
Planning Step I: Selecting the behavior to be changed

1. What ONE behavior will you work on first? Notice the word 'ONE'. When you arrive at this stage with a student, usually there are several behaviors that need "adjusting." If anyone's safety or rights are involved, you have no choice, you must start there. Otherwise, you have a choice of the most important behavior (such as not learning), the most annoying behaviors (such as smart remarks), or a behavior that is relatively easy to change (such as raising hands instead of blurting out answers — yes, that is easy to change)!

Often, it is wise to start with an easy behavior so you and the student will experience quick success or with an annoying behavior so you get relief. In either case, you will learn from your efforts and will have a better notion of what may work with a more difficult behavior.

Sometimes you may decide to list the behaviors that need changing and, in the subsequent conference, let the student select the one where (s)he would like to begin. Again, this accords the student the dignity of being the decision maker and indicates your confidence in his/her ability to choose.

Planning Step II: Determining the replacement behavior

You can't expect a student to stop doing something unless you help him/her learn to do something else in its place. That "something" must be predictably possible for the student at this point in time, not in the eventual future.

At times, the replacement behavior is obvious. Raising a hand and waiting to be called on replaces calling out. Keeping a smart remark to oneself or making a productive contribution replaces wise cracking. But what replaces hitting when one is angry? Ignoring the other person is not initially possible for a hitter. Using your mouth instead of your hands may be possible and you can clean up the language later. Finishing all assignments for a student who never finishes anything may be a laudable *long term* goal, but finishing one abbreviated assignment is possible and will yield more immediate success. A *realistic* replacement behavior needs to be specified so you know whether your strategy is working.

Planning Step III: Determining positive reinforcers

List the reinforcers you think might work for this student and select the "smallest" one. If it doesn't work, you will have "bigger" ones to try. If a verbal reinforcer that commends a student's effort and competence will work, "Bill, you're really trying and you're getting better and better," don't use the "big guns" of rewards and privileges which tend to be more addictive.

Sometimes, in the conference which results from this planning, you will let the student select or determine the reinforcers. Their choices can be very revealing.

Planning Step IV: Selecting negative reinforcers or consequences

Sinners don't turn into saints overnight, so you need to make plans for the times when the unacceptable behavior emerges in order both to suppress it and to give a clear message that it will not be ignored. Ignoring it (extinction) will not work when behavior reaches the point of necessitating a private conference. Whenever possible, use a negative reinforcer so you leave the student in charge. Whenever the student decides to change behavior, (s)he can remove the negative reinforcer. A punishment leaves the teacher in charge as only (s)he can remove it. Punishment is sometimes necessary, and the *memory* of a previous punishment can become a subsequent negative reinforcer: "When I talked, the teacher made me stay after school. I don't want to stay after school, so I can remove that possibility by not talking."

Frequently, a student's parents can become effective negative reinforcers. This does not mean using parents in a negative way. "Sue, when you have a problem at home, are your parents helpful in solving it?" Sue answers a hesitant, "Sometimes." "Would it help if your parents came to school and helped on this problem?" This time there is no hesitation in Sue's emphatic "No." "OK, I don't think you need them. I think you can handle it."

Note that Sue can remove the aversive stimulus of her parents coming to school by eliminating the problem behavior. Her dignity is maintained because she is in charge.

It's a very different message when you say, "If you don't straighten up, I'll send for your parents." While the outcome may be that same, the

Message is, "I suspect you won't do it and I'll have to send for your parents. Sue's dignity and feelings of competence can be destroyed.

Planning Step V: Determining what might help the student use the desired behavior

At first it may be necessary to assist with, while you insist on the replacement behavior. Plan for ways to cue or prompt the behavior. "Don't say anything, but raise your hand if you are ready to answer the question," with a signal from your eyes can help a "blurter outer." Being out on the yard when the bell rings and walking in with the typically tardy student may get her in on time. Frequent checking and reinforcing: "That one is just right. I'll be back in a minute to see how many more you have done," may speed up a dawdler. Separating a student from a distraction may help him focus. Remember, the job of a teacher is to help students "do right" not to catch them "doing wrong."

Planning Step VI: Determining whether to include others in the conference

It is often helpful to have another professional (principal, counselor, the student's former teacher) think through these planning steps with you. Two heads are frequently better than one. In the actual conference, usually it is conducted with only teacher and student. Save the "others" in case you need them later. If the problem involves others (behavior in the cafeteria, on the bus, with the aide), those people should be present in the conference so the student does not have the opportunity to "play the ends against the middle" and there is no lack of understanding among everyone involved.

Occasionally, it is effective to present a "formidable array" of authority figures, principal, assistant principal, coach, noon yard aids, parents, and teacher so the student knows everyone is hearing the same message and there will be no subsequent misunderstandings. Usually this occurs when a previous conference hasn't worked.

All of these planning steps add up to the strategy for the conference (lesson) which has high probability for changing student behavior for the better. This planning is culminated in the procedures for conducting the conferences.

CONDUCTING THE CONFERENCE

Resist the impulse to deliver a moral lecture. The conference should be focussed on future behavior not past sins.

I. Identify and Label the Unacceptable Behavior

Begin by identifying the problem. Usually the student can do it. "Tom, why are we meeting?" If you get "I don't know," you need to decide whether to read from your record or let the student think until he decides to remember it. Conferencing is the same as teaching in that there is no "right way." It depends on student and situation.

Regardless of who says it, the important outcome is that the unacceptable behavior is specified in behavioral terms, not just categories. "Not taking turns" is specific. "Selfish" is not. "Making humming noises" is specific. "Disturbing the class" is not. "Working without arguing with your group" is specific. "Cooperating" is not.

II. Identify the Specific Replacement Behavior

Not only must the student know precisely the behavior to be changed, with many specific examples, but also must learn the appropriate replacement behavior with several examples plus practice in using them. The inappropriate behavior has occurred many times or you would not be holding the conference so it is habitual behavior. Frequently, students are *told* to stop doing something, but are not *taught* how to start using the acceptable behavior in its place and given practice in simulated situations.

Remember, what the student is to do must be predictably possible for that student *at this time* — not at a future time when (s)he has completely reformed.

In the conference, role playing often is effective so the teacher can see if the student possesses the skills necessary to actually practice the replacement behavior. The teacher asks a question. The student raises a hand and *waits* until the teacher calls on her. The student makes the annoying noise. The teacher gives the agreed upon signal and the student stops the noise. The student makes a statement. The teacher disagrees. The student defends his point of view and then stops without arguing further (This does not mean a student should not defend an opinion, the practice is for a "chronic arguer" who argues about every direction). The teacher or a best friend calls the student the name the student has indicated makes him / her mad and the student practices acceptable responses in place of hitting. The teacher presents a situation where the student feels unfairly treated and the student practices acceptable ways of discussing it.

Sometimes, the teacher will find the student really doesn't have the words to use or skills necessary for the replacement behavior. Those words or skills need to be taught, modeled, and "mass practiced" before they can become stronger and more readily available than the old, possibly practiced-for-years behavior.

III. Indicate the Future Consequences of Unacceptable and of Replacement Behaviors

Usually, the student should know the consequences of both kinds of behaviors so (s)he is aware that (s)he has a choice and is the one who will determine which will occur. It is critical that students realize that they are in charge of their behaviors and, when they know the consequences, they are making a choice to behave in a certain way, therefore, they control what happens. They need to learn that they are originators, not pawns, of most (not all) of what happens to them.

Occasionally, it is more impressive for the student not to know "what will happen if you do it again." This is useful when you feel that sometimes the circumstance will differ and therefore consequences should differ (we do this even for murder). Sometimes the student may be goaded beyond endurance and hit, may be so excited she fails to raise her hand, may be so motivated he shoves. While these times are few, we should always consider the circumstances surrounding the problem. That's why we're professionals, not robots. Obviously, lack of consistency depending on our mood does not qualify as a reason for changing consequences.

IV. Set Time for Checking Success of Plan

At the conference, a date should be set to determine the success of the plan. For serious behaviors, the next period or day should be the first check point so success can be reinforced immediately and consequences imposed for lack of success. Remember, knowledge of results, "How am I doing?" is an effective motivator.

Some behaviors may need a few days to "get going" before they are checked. Don't let much time elapse, however, or you'll lose your momentum and the student may not feel accountable

V. Record Agreements

Recording is impressive and always signifies that something is important. The conference is no exception. A formal summary record of (1) the problem, (2) the replacement behavior, (3) the consequences, and (4) times for checking success needs to be formalized. You may use an official form (see page 84) or an "impressive" sheet of paper, dated and signed by student, teacher, and any other person present. As with any contract, the student should have a copy and the original be stored in an "official file" so there is no possibility of its being misplaced or unavailable.

VI. Put Plan into Action

Don't wait for the ultimate, perfect solution. Start, then make modifications if, subsequently, they are indicated. You may find you were expecting too much or too little and need to adjust the replacement behavior. Your anticipated reinforcers may not be effective and you may need to use "stronger" ones. You may experiences easy success or discouraging failure. Remember, you can always redesign the strategy and, with the help of good theory, *almost* always solve the problem.

BEHAVIOR STRATEGY FORM

Date _____ Name of student or group _____

Adults involved _____

Date for strategy to begin _____

1. ONE BEHAVIOR What is the one behavior you want to change?	
2. REPLACEMENT BEHAVIOR Identify the behavior that is to take its place.	
3. POSITIVE REINFORCEMENT Determine the positive reinforcers needed or desired by this student or group that will take place when the appropriate behavior is exhibited.	
4. NEGATIVE REINFORCEMENT Determine appropriate negative reinforcers that are not desired by this student or group that will be most effective in this case.	
5. RECORD Do you need a base line? How will you record improvement?	
6. THE PLAN Conference: Who needs to be involved?	
Success: What will you do to insure success (prompt, role play, change seat, lower – of problems, etc.)?	
Follow up: When and how will you follow up? When will you reevaluate to determine if modifications or revisions are needed?	

Let's practice by trying these psychological principles on the student who is a constant talker in the classroom. (Does this remind you of one of yours?) What is the first thing we need to do?

a. Extinguish the response

.....................................Turn to page 86 (a).

b. Negatively reinforce or punish

.....................................Turn to page 86 (b).

c. Positively reinforce

.....................................Turn to page 86 (c).

d. Identify the behavior to be changed

.....................................Turn to page 86 (d).

a. You said we would extinguish the response.

Don't we wish it! You extinguish a response by ignoring it and the only thing that ignoring constant talking will accomplish for us is best described by our psychiatrist. The talking habit is too pervasive to extinguish, it will continue unless we do something. Go back to the question on page 85 and choose something the teacher can do that will produce more productive results.

b. You said we would negatively reinforce or punish talking.

We may need to, but how is the student going to know if we are blasting her for talking, not working, disturbing her neighbors, or irritating us? Go back to the question on page 85 and choose an answer that will leave no question in her mind as to what behavior needs to be changed.

c. You said we should positively reinforce him.

It would take a saint to overlook the fact that he is constantly running off at the mouth. We may be able to give him positive reinforcement in some areas but not for control of his vocal chords. Go back to the question on page 85 and choose an answer that will put some responsibility on him.

d. You said we should identify the behavior to be changed.

Absolutely correct! He needs to know what we are concerned about and why. Here again the skilled teacher gets him to think through the problem (Don't be surprised if he really believes he should not talk because we don't like it). Remember our technique of recording the frequency of the response (the number of times a day that he is talking when he should not). This will help him focus on the severity of the problem and establish a base line for computing growth. Now let us go to the next step of our plan for changing his behavior.

Turn to the next page.

Our habitual talker has identified her problem behavior and resolved to do something about it. How do we help her keep from falling right back into her old talking habit?

a. We identify it for her
...............................Turn to page 88 (a).

b. We negatively reinforce it
...............................Turn to page 88 (b).

c. We positively reinforce it
...............................Turn to page 88 (c).

d. We extinguish it
...............................Turn to page 88 (d).

a. You said we identify it for her.

We just did, or rather, if we were skilled, she did it for herself. Now that she knows what the problem is, go back to the question on page 87 and see what we can do to help.

b. We negatively reinforce it.

You bet we do! We want that talking suppressed. We might signal her when she is doing it. If that does not work, we can walk over, get a piece of paper, and record it. All of this, of course, without anyone else knowing that plan. It is strictly a private matter between you and the student and nobody else's business. If we need to make our negative reinforcer stronger, we put a tally mark on the board without letting the rest of the class know why. The culprit is really going to seek a response (which is to stop talking) that will take that action (negative reinforcer) away before the rest catch on to what you are tallying. So, you are in business. Negative reinforcement has suppressed the response (talking that brought it on and strengthened the response (not talking) that takes it away.

We, again, need to warn you that if some undesirable response, such as daydreaming, removes the negative reinforcer, that response will be strengthened. So watch out!

Now turn to page 89.

c. You said we positively reinforce talking.

You are correct if you positively reinforce *not* talking. But if you positively reinforce talking, you must be kidding or else you are getting ready to resign and let someone else cope with her. Go back to the question on page 87 and choose an answer that will cause her to talk less.

d. You said we extinguish it.

Eventually we have to, but right now the habit of talking is much too strong to die by itself. Doing nothing simply means we are admitting that there is nothing we can do and we are not at that point. Go back to page 87 and choose an answer that will show her that talking needs to stop.

We have helped our talker identify her problem behavior. We have negatively reinforced talking behavior so her talking is suppressed and not talking is strengthened by positive reinforcers. Now what can we do to be sure she spends increasing time in a "not talking" (and consequently listening and learning) state?

a. We switch to an intermittent schedule

. . . . Turn to page 90 (a).

b. We extinguish her talking

. . . . Turn to page 90 (b).

c. We use negative reinforcers

. . . . Turn to page 90 (c).

d. We use positive reinforcers

. . . . Turn to page 90 (d).

a. You said we switch to an intermittent schedule.

You are on the right track but ahead of yourself. Her not-talking-listening-and-learning response is new and not strong enough yet to be more probable than her habitual talking response. Go back to page 89 and choose an answer that will strengthen the response that needs to become more frequent.

b. You said we extinguish her talking.

It is a step we may eventually take but she is not ready for it yet. She is still not sure this "not talking" is really going to pay off. Go back to page 89 and choose a response that will convince her it is the way to the good life at school.

c. You said we use negative reinforcers.

We have already done this. Of course maybe you are so fed up with her you would like to do it again but now we need to move to the next step. Go back to the question on page 89 and choose an answer that will increase that more productive behavior we want to strengthen.

d. You said we should use positive reinforcers.

You are absolutely right! Now, whenever she is quietly working or listening, we need to do something so she knows this is the way it should be. Excusing her first because she has worked so quietly, praising her business-like way of handling school work, writing her mother a note telling her what a wonderful girl she has, or "accusing" her of never giving you an opportunity to scold any more, all may be effective reinforcers depending on you, the student, and the situation. Once is not enough, but again, and again, and again she has to be reinforced on a continuous schedule until the new working and listening behavior becomes stronger than the old talking behavior.

Now turn to the next page.

Now that you have a quiet worker, do you have to keep praising her the rest of his life so she won't slip back? Not if you:

a. Record her success

. . . . .Turn to page 92 (a).

b. Change to an intermittent schedule

. . . . .Turn to page 92 (b).

c. Make working quietly habitual

. . . . .Turn to page 92 (c).

d. Let her know that is what you expect

. . . . .Turn to page 92 (d).

a. You said we should record her success.

We hope you have already done it. That is an important positive reinforcer and is technically known as *knowledge of results*. It will certainly tend to strengthen her response, but go back to page 91 and choose an answer that will keep her from slipping back into old habits.

b. You said we should change to an intermittent schedule.

Absolutely! You remembered that once we established a productive response by continuous reinforcers we needed to change to an intermittent schedule to make "not talking" resistant to forgetting. You recall we skipped reinforcing one time and then went back to it, skipped more times and went back, etc. It is like a review with the intervals between practice getting longer and longer. It really works!

Now turn to page 93.

c. You said we make working quietly habitual.

That we do, but how? Go back to the question on page 91 and choose an answer that will make working quietly resistant to forgetting.

d. You said we let her know that is what we expect.

Other teachers have tried this and you got the results of their labors. That should be enough to make you go back to page 91 and choose a different answer.

Let's practice with Peter who habitually is a clown in class. He uses his skill to get attention, make people laugh, and break up the class at the times he desires. You are tempted to "break him up" but your professional training (thank goodness) tells you that (a) he wishes attention, (b) he has been successful in getting it by clowning, (c) he probably does not get it by other methods (or he would be using them), (d) he may be clowning as behavior to cope with situations he cannot handle in any other way, i.e., he does not know the right answer to the question you ask, or (e) because he is not popular, he does not think he will get attention from the group in any other way.

He obviously has his needs but you have yours — and an orderly controlled classroom with no clowns is rightfully one of them. Letting him continue clowning may make him successful for the moment, but it is not a productive coping mechanism, and we have a responsibility for helping him develop a better one.

The number one step in changing his behavior is to let him know in a conference that you will:

a. Help him identify the behavior to be changed
. . . . Turn to page 94 (a).

b. Ignore the clowning
. . . . Turn to page 94 (b).

c. Punish the clowning
. . . . Turn to page 95 (c).

d. Positively reinforce his good behavior
. . . . Turn to page 95 (d).

a. You said the first step is to help him identify the behavior to be changed.

Perfect! You are on your way! He needs to have his old habit brought to a conscious level. (His typical response when you reprimand him is, "What did *I* do? I just said....") But remember, when you say, "Stop clowning," you need to get him to decide what he should start doing. If the new response ("Start helping with your good ideas") is incompatible with the old response (clowning), then one has to replace the other and you have really changed behavior. It is no use working with responses that could happen together (clowning while giving right answers) because one does not have to replace the other.

This step sounds easy but it is not. The trick is to have *him* identify the problem and suggest solutions to it. Your *telling* him what he should do will just be another episode in a long series of unsuccessful attempts by well-meaning (but psychologically uninformed) people. It also helps if he knows the frequency with which this behavior is occurring. ("Peter, were you aware that this happened six times today?" Let's keep track of the number of times it happens tomorrow so we'll know how much of a habit it is.") Not only has the problems been identified, but you have established a way of measuring growth in behavior. When clowning occurs less, you know you are on the right track. If you don't realize he has reduced it from a six to one incidence, you are apt to be vulnerable to that there-he-goes-again feeling. This was a long way of saying, "Your answer was absolutely correct"; so turn now to page 96 for the second step in our reformation of Peter.

b. You said to ignore the clowning.

If this were the first time it happened, you would be absolutely correct, but this is behavior of long standing. Ignoring it will probably convince Peter and the class that you feel helpless about the possibility of doing anything about it. Turn back to the question on page 93 and choose an answer that will be easier on your blood pressure.

c. You said to punish the clowning.

You are on the right track, but you are ahead of yourself. You need to make sure that Peter is aware of what it is about his behavior that is unacceptable and what to do which *is* acceptable to get attention. If you scold or glare, he will get the attention he desired, and it will be difficult to determine whether you are mad at him or at the class for laughing at him. If you were Peter which would you choose to think? Go back to the question on page 93 and decide the first thing you need to do.

d. You said to positively reinforce his good behavior.

We hope you do. But if you are a wise teacher, you have been doing that right along and he is still clowning. This is a time when just emphasizing the positive will not work. He is getting too much satisfaction from his clowning behavior. Go back to the question on page 93 and choose an answer that will interrupt the behavior pattern he has developed and help him acquire a better one.

After Peter has identified his problem as clowning and, from your record, acknowledges he uses this technique often each day, what can we do next that will most effectively change his behavior? (Remember, when a student stops doing one thing he has to start doing something else.)

a. Punish the clowning

. . . . Turn to page 98 (a).

b. Extinguish the clowning

. . . . Turn to page 98 (b).

c. Positively reinforce some behavior incompatible with clowning

. . . . Turn to page 98 (c).

d. Ridicule him for clowning

. . . . Turn to page 98 (d).

a. You said we should punish the clowning.

That would be a good way to say, "Stop clowning!" But what is he to start doing? He needs to have a desirable alternative to the response that he knows best. If the new response is something he cannot do when he clowns, you have the answer. Turn back to the question on page 97 and pick an answer that will do just that.

b. You said we should extinguish the clowning.

Eventually, we may need to, but before we can do that, he will have to develop a better response that he can use when he feels the urge to clown to get attention. Go back to the question on page 97 and choose an answer that incorporates this idea.

c. You said we should positively reinforce some behavior incompatible with the clowning.

Right you are! If he develops some new behavior such as giving serious answers or furthering class discussion, we can give him attention with heavy positive reinforcers to make this kind of response more probable than the clowning response. Eventually, we may have to extinguish the clowning response by letting it come out reinforced, but we want to be sure his acceptable response has been reinforced enough to be more probable.

Now turn to page 99.

d. You said we should ridicule him for clowning.

This action might tend to suppress the clowning but it also would give him attention from us and sympathy from the class. Ridicule, causing a student to lose dignity is not helpful. Besides, he only knows what not to do. He hasn't identified what an acceptable behavior is so he can practice it and we can reinforce it. Go back to the question on page 97 and choose an answer that incorporates this idea.

Now that Peter knows he will be rewarded with praise and attention when he gives serious answers that further class discussion, in order to be sure his acceptable response is more probable, we should:

a. Plan situations where he will respond well and praise him every time he does

.................................Turn to page 100 (a).

b. Negatively reinforce him when he clowns

.................................Turn to page 100 (b).

c. Change to an intermittent schedule of praise when he gives serious answers

.................................Turn to page 100 (c).

a. You said we should plan situations where he will respond well and praise him every time he does.

You are absolutely right. So we alert him to the question we are going to ask and that he may be called on to give the explanation to the class or he may be the teacher and call on someone else to give the answers and tell them whether or not they are right.

Turn to the next page..

b. You said we should punish him when he clowns.

We may not need to. We will have to see first whether or not we can teach the new response without suppressing the clowning response. Turn back to the question on page 99 and select an answer that will help him quickly learn the appropriate response.

c. You said we should change to an intermittent schedule of praise when he gives serious answers.

Eventually, we will need to, but he is not ready for that yet, because we are not sure his serious answers are more probable than his clowning behavior. Go back to the question on page 99 and select an answer that will make his new behavior stronger.

CHAPTER IX
STRATEGIES FOR CHANGING BEHAVIOR

Now, let's translate all this theory and practice into some strategies you can use in a classroom or in the total school program to encourage students to become productively in charge of their own behavior: to be self disciplined.

Let's begin with some teaching behaviors that will help start students toward satisfying self discipline at the beginning of the school year.

First, list five productive behaviors you hope each of your students will exhibit. These will be the behaviors you will reinforce from the minute the students enter your class. The reason we suggest five is that (1) those will be the most important and you won't get bogged in trying to remember a long list of desirable but less essential (to you, at this time) behaviors and (2) you can keep those few important behaviors in mind and can be consistent in your reinforcing of them. As those are achieved, you can add others. The following are frequently listed:

Coming to class on time
Having necessary materials
Raising hands
Listening courteously
Finishing work
Speaking politely
Working quietly
Making contributions to class
Behaving appropriately at breaks
Doing homework
Doing extended thinking or quality work
Helping others
Doing neat and accurate work
Doing special or extra projects
Following rules and directions
Waiting for turns
Helping others
Paying attention

Keeping area clean
Behaving appropriately in assemblies, cafeteria, and on the yard

Many people feel that students will be more cooperative if they set their own rules in a democratic way. That's fine, but it's not democracy because students know they can't set the "rule" that they can leave class whenever they wish, they can't "vote" homework out of existence, they can't "legalize" eating or talking in class whenever they want to. So, if you wish students to "make their own rules," go ahead, but know they are usually recalling and "listing" the rules they know are acceptable to you. It is the author's experience that as long as rules are fair and just, students don't care who makes them. So, do whatever is comfortable for you.

Begin reinforcing productive behaviors as soon as students enter class. The author observed an excellent teacher on the first day of school. The students entered talking and laughing with their friends, chatted with the teacher and followed the directions on the chalkboard, "Sit in any place you wish."

The bell rang and the teacher walked up to the front of the room. (Remember, it's the first day.) Talking stopped and the students looked expectantly at the teacher. She "put" a surprised look on her face and exclaimed, "You're mind readers! How did you know that when I come up to the front of the room it's the signal that we're going to begin? Almost everyone's eyes are on me." (What do you think the students whose eyes were elsewhere are now doing?) "You'll find you understand better if you watch the speaker's face whether it's a teacher, guest speaker, student, or the principal. A person's face and hand movements add information to what the person is saying. It's great that most of your hands are empty. You'll find that having things in your hands sends messages to your brain that distract you from what you're hearing." (What do you think the students are doing who were playing with objects?) "Many of you are sitting with a friend. You were talking and laughing before the bell rang. Now you're listening and not being distracted by or distracting your friend. This is going to a great class. You're really in charge of yourselves."

That teacher is setting rules: (1) Stop talking when I go to the front of the class, (2) Put your eyes on me and get rid of things in your hands, and (3) Listen carefully and don't talk to your neighbor when I'm talking. But she's doing it all with positive reinforcer messages that convey, "You're competent, putting forth effort, and are worthy — a great class."

Quite different teaching behavior from posting a set of rules ("Now, these are the rules in the class.") which can encourage some "creative" individuals to start inventing ways they can bypass them. If you wish to list rules, do so, but teach and reinforce them so the posted list is no longer needed after the first few weeks of school. We don't leave the multiplication facts up all year, students learn them. The same goes for rules.

Teaching a Signal for Attention

A second important beginning strategy is to establish a signal that means, "Stop, look, listen, and don't go back to work until the signal is off." Teachers may choose the signal or students can "elect" one. The signal can be a sound, lights, chime, voice, whatever. Our preference is the teacher's voice as that is always available to the teacher. "Class," "Attention please," or "Signal's on" are some examples, "Signal's on" and "Signal's off" have the advantage of positive transfer from stop lights.

Then, the teacher needs to teach (not tell) students how to respond to the signal. To do this the teacher will use the same principles of practice that produce automaticity with times tables, spelling, and athletics. The following is an example of how it might be (not should be) done.

"Class, there are times when I need to give you important information. To alert you to those times so you don't miss something essential, I'm going to say, 'Signal's on.' That means you stop what you're doing, get things out of your hands so they don't distract you, put your eyes on me, and listen carefully to what I say because it will be important for you. Don't go back to work until I say, 'Signal's off.' Let's practice that. Pretend you are writing. Signal's on. Great, almost everyone looked up immediately." (For those who didn't the teacher is trying extinction.) "Let's make it harder. Talk softly to your friend. (Pause) Signal's on! Super, most of you were able to stop yourself and look up. That's great. Now let's start our work. Open your book to page 82, read that page, and be ready with a question that would test whether someone understood it. (Pause) Signal's on! You're really alert. I can't catch most of you even when you're concentrating on something else. Now we'll start to work on our _____ and I'll see if I can catch you later in the period. But you've learned the signal so fast I'll bet you'll remember what to do."

Not being "caught" is a positive reinforcer to most of us. It means we are astute, alert, and not easily tricked. However, when the teacher uses the possibility of being caught as a reinforcer (s)he had better be pretty sure the students will not be caught, otherwise it becomes a "put down."

The teacher will use "Signal's on" several times in the first period it is taught. At the end of the period (s)he needs to warn students it will be used again the next period and "don't get caught." The following period the signal will be used several times (massed practice) decreasing (intermittent practice) over several days until it is habitual (automatic) behavior.

Most students will respond productively but there always are a few who are going to "try out teacher." At first, ignoring them is the best policy along with reinforcing a student who is sitting close by and who obeyed the signal. "Paul you looked so engrossed in what you were doing but when I said, 'Signal's on,' you immediately looked up. You're really alert!" Often reinforcing a neighbor will bring a "sinner into the fold."

If this doesn't work, try a private prompt, "Mary, in just a minute I'm going to give the signal. Be ready to stop and look up." If she does, look directly at her so she knows the message is for her as you say, "Most of you are doing a great job of stopping yourselves and looking up the minute you hear the signal." Avoid using her name in your reinforcer. "Mary was one of the first to look up," tells her your reinforcers are phoney because you prompted her. Your eyes can convey the message of appreciation.

Sometimes *this* doesn't work. Nothing always works! In that case you have to give additional individual prompting. Well taught, however, signals require very little individual accommodation.

For the student for whom none of the above works (and there are a few of them), a private conference is indicated. "Betty, I need to see you for a minute after class. Be thinking why." Then, after the rest of the group have been dismissed, sit down for your conference so the student knows this is no causal encounter.

"Betty, have you thought why we needed to talk?" If she has, you have something to reinforce. "I was sure you were aware of it." If not, simply take the lead by, "Whenever I say 'Signal's on' you have a hard time stopping what you're doing and looking at me." (Remember, you retain her dignity.) Let's practice that now so I'm sure I have made myself clear." Practice a couple of times and then conclude with, "Next period I am going to tally how may times you look up when I give the signal." (Record the positive instances of looking up, leave blanks by the recorded signal if she doesn't look up.) "At the end of the period we'll examine your record. Will it help if I give you a cue before I say 'Signal's on'? I'll be happy to do that if you think it will help." This gives her the message, "You will do it, how can I help?"

Whatever arrangements are made, follow through with a brief accounting conference at the end of class so Betty knows you are serious. "Betty, you did a great job (did better). I'll bet you'll need fewer reminders tomorrow." For some students, this is enough. For others, it may take a few days before they realize you really mean it.

"Who has time for all of this?" you ask. Taking time to get productive behavior at the beginning saves countless hours of time for the rest of the year. Then you can concentrate on the academic curriculum because little time is needed for student management problems.

Because you feel committed to teach academic content, you frequently are tempted to use the signal and then proceed with instructions even though a few students have not obeyed the signal. Resist that temptation! There is no way that is more sure to let students know you don't mean it than proceeding without requiring attention from everyone. Often you can "bring in the strays" by saying, "Almost everyone is ready," or "We'll wait for two more people to look up." No names should be mentioned, you won't need to. Sometimes standing by the student and touching the desk when you give the signal indicates you mean it.

The same basic strategy of teaching a behavior, then reinforcing that behavior will work for any behavior you wish students to exhibit. Bringing materials, being on time, doing homework, raising hands, working productively by oneself or in a cooperative group, cleaning up and replacing materials are all learned behaviors which can be systematically taught (not admonished), practiced, and reinforced so they become automatic and need only an occasional reinforcer.

This strategy also works for critical thinking, creativity, and productive decision making as well as for academic, artistic, and psychomotor learning, but those behaviors are not the subject of this book. If you transfer what you have learned in this book to those "higher level" behaviors, you will be amazed by how much more probable and frequent those behaviors will also become.

Cafeteria (Yard, Hall, Bus, Assembly) Behavior

Cafeteria, yard, hall, bus, and assembly behaviors are behaviors which can be improved by use of systematic strategies. The following are examples of what might be (not should be) done.

One teacher remarked, "If I'm not good, when I die and go to Hades, I'll be on permanent cafeteria duty!" Such a prediction is not unfounded. Whenever large groups gather, adults or children, there can be problems of behavior, noise, and confusion. To minimize such problems, the school staff needs to agree upon and *be accountable for teaching and supporting* certain standards of cafeteria (yard, bus, hall, assembly) behaviors.

To have a silent cafeteria is unrealistic and smacks of prison expectations. To have a cafeteria where you can hold a conversation with the person next to you without shouting, and food is handled as it should be, is the result of excellent teaching.

This teaching begins with a classroom discussion of agreed upon cafeteria rules and the reasons they are important (*real* reasons, not parroted ones). "Noise and confusion make people tired and cross. That's why we have acoustic tile in the cafeteria and routines for picking up and returning dishes and trays as well as disposing of paper, plastic and leftover food. Let's go over the ways we can act to eliminate unpleasant results from noise and confusion."

Then teachers TEACH by accompanying students to the cafeteria, *practicing* getting trays, sitting down to eat, returning trays and utensils, speaking in a way that the other end of the table cannot hear you. During this practice, there are teacher annotations of appropriate behavior with specific knowledge of results to students.

"Bill is sitting by his friend and talking but we, at this end of the table aren't hearing what he is saying. That means his voice level is appropriate."

"Tom is waiting until his mouth is empty before he asks Mary a question."

"Mary is putting her napkin in the waste basket before she puts her tray on the rack."

"What is Susan doing that makes our cafeteria a more pleasant place?"

Obviously, our words fit the age and maturity of the students. What would be appropriate for third graders would be insulting to high school students. The latter, however, also need supervised, *annotated* practice so behavioral expectations are articulated, observed and practiced in the same way as we set procedures and practice in fire drills and in academic work. We know that students learn academics faster when we annotate successful practice. "Notice the first thing Tom is doing in solving the equation (selecting the subject, reading the map)." Annotation is also important in learning self discipline.

Any new learning needs first to be practiced under guidance. If the cafeteria is disorderly, appropriate behavior is new learning. Yes, we know they "should be able to do it" but they haven't been, so we need to *teach* and they need to *practice* with teacher guidance. Usually, aides are not trained to give the quality of guidance needed. Once behavior is learned and desirable patterns set, aides may be able to maintain those patterns.

Consequently, it is necessary for teachers to be with students in the cafeteria for a few days so those students who need it experience accountability and, if necessary, consequences for inappropriate behavior. At first, having students sit at the same place each day makes identification of trouble spots easy. Sitting where one pleases can become a privilege earned by responsible behavior. Not eating in the cafeteria can become a reasonable consequence related to irresponsible behavior while there. Recording *group* (not individual) growth in some observable ways (charts, privileges) gives students reinforcing knowledge.

We are well aware of teachers' need for a relaxing, pupil-free lunch period. "Donating" some time to get a cafeteria in order will pay large dividends later as complaints, disorder, and upset-after-lunch classes diminish or disappear. Often it is possible for one or two volunteer teachers to assume daily cafeteria duty initially while they are relieved of some other responsibility. We know the effects of a series of different substitute teachers on classroom learning. The same effect occurs in the cafeteria, when supervision and behavioral expectations constantly change. Before long, with consistent supervision, the cafeteria will be in good order and behavioral expectations can be maintained by an aide.

This same procedure of teaching expected behaviors, practicing, monitoring, and reinforcing them will result in success on the yard, halls, bus, assembly or anywhere else.

Students Who Don't Do Their Work

One of the most frustrating situations for a teacher to encounter is students who don't do an assignment that the teacher believes is possible and justified. The first question to be asked, before we consider ways of getting them to do it is, "Could the reason be that the assignment is too difficult so the student *can't* do it, or that the assignment is too easy so the student doesn't need to do it?"

"But they *should* be able to do it if they are in this class," is no excuse for assigning a task that the student, with effort, can't do. Equally indefensible is the statement, "But a student should assume responsibility for doing homework whether it is needed or not." We agree that assuming responsibility for tasks is a trait all students need to develop but it can be developed more readily when the task is something needing to be done. Think of your attitude should you be required to complete a page of reading and respond to questions or do math problems that you already know how to do, or work on questions or problems when you don't know what to do. Have you ever wondered about the logic of the statement, "(S)he got perfect scores on every test but I had to give him / her a 'B' because (s)he didn't turn in homework?" The answer is not, "*No* homework," but is homework that gives practice really *needed* by that student in order to do a perfect test.

Some teachers may believe it is unfair to give different homework to students in the same class. Nothing is more unfair than to treat very different students as if they were the same. Students see assignments as "fair and just" when they reflect differing learning needs. When we are developing students' bodies, they do *some* of the same exercises and *some* that are custom tailored to their needs. Should we do less for their minds?

If you have ascertained that students *can* do the assignment and *need* to do it, the next question becomes, "Have they had the opportunity to do it?" If classroom time is allocated, the opportunity is there. If the assignment is homework, work or family demands could interfere, so time at school may need to be allocated. We realize that school work usually is more important to students' future, but the immediacy of needing to care for younger siblings, do family chores, earn money or the lure of friends and television can take priority.

Remember, the only time we control is school time, but we may exert a lot of influence on out of school time and intentions by making assignments interesting and short. More is learned in a short, highly motivated practice assignment by a ''reason for doing it'' than a long one where attention and motivation drag.

Giving students who consistently finish practice assignments an occasional time in class where they can do an extra credit assignment or work on anything they choose *without* feeling guilty because they aren't working for extra credit, can reinforce turning in homework. ''Time off for good behavior'' is a reinforcer for most people in our society.

In the same ''free period,'' the teacher needs to work with students who haven't turned in homework, encouraging them to display their competence and reinforcing it. ''Why should we reinforce students who haven't done what they were supposed to?'' some may ask. ''Because we want them to start doing it. Reinforcing them while they *are* doing it has the highest probability for getting them to continue,'' is the professional's answer.

Assignments may need to be shortened *temporarily* for students who are needing to assume responsibility for self direction. In the same way that you need to learn to do simple math or writing before you can do a complex assignment of either, you need to learn to complete a short assignment before you are accountable for a long one. ''But they should be able to'' may be correct but it is obvious that they, at this point in time, are not able to direct themselves to complete the long assignment. Directing themselves to complete ''a few'' is growth over completing none. When they have accomplished ''those few,'' more can be added, making sure that ''more of the same'' is really needed. If students can do a few examples correctly, do they really need to do a page of the same? Why not work on something else that needs learning?

Occasionally, losing break time before or after school, or special occasions may be necessary to convince students that meeting expectations is more desirable than not meeting them. If this, or any other consequence used over time does not work, don't continue using it.

There may be a few students who don't do work to get attention (we certainly give it to them) or to ''bug'' the teacher or parents. In these few cases, let students know that you are aware of what is happening and from now on you will neither expect nor look at their work. If they want to learn or not learn it is up to them, you are no longer involved and *then stick to non-involvement* for a period long enough to give extinction a chance to work. If possible, enlist the parents in the same extinction of a student's nonproductive attention seeking response. Ignoring a student's non-working bid for attention is not easy but when it is successfully done, it frequently works wonders.

Inappropriate Language

Some students use language that is inappropriate at school. We cannot say it is "bad language" because what is inappropriate in one situation (school) may be considered appropriate in another (home, street, club, team) where it is used by parents or friends.

We should simply label such language as "inappropriate." "You would not wear your bathing suit or only your undershorts to school. That is not an acceptable way of dressing here although there are places where it is OK. In the same way, those words you are using are inappropriate at school. Let's think of some words you might use in their place to express your feelings."

Remember, if you stop doing one thing, you need to start doing something else in its place. It's an excellent opportunity to teach vocabulary — "incorrigible," "exasperating," "disgusting," "ignorant," "unintelligent," "pettifogging," or any words that will express the students' feelings while building vocabulary.

While you would prefer the student use no derogatory words, that degree of control may not be possible at this time. Better to begin with reasonably acceptable words which are learned and used in place of unacceptable ones.

Before the conference with the student (or with the class for this may be a class problem), the unacceptable words need to be listed. If the list is recorded and communicated there is no mistake as to what the unacceptable words are. (One girl asked the author in amazement, "My God, Dr. Hunter, is even 'damn' swearing?") Making an observable list of unacceptable "four letter words" is an impressive, deterring act in itself.

Next, the student needs to practice using replacement words in simulated situations that have high probability of eliciting the unacceptable words (someone calling him/her a name, something not going well). Remember, we don't expect a student to learn a new math procedure without guided practice. The same is true of any new behavior or response.

No learned behavior changes overnight, so we should not expect it of inappropriate language. A few slips are to be expected. Consequently, we may ask the student to estimate the amount of time it will take to eliminate *all* unacceptable words. We insist, however, that over time there must be a steady escalation of acceptable language. This acknowledges the fact that there could be unintentional "slips" but that steady and measurable progress is expected.

Reinforcing successful periods, (recess, noon break, class periods when there have been no infractions) while, at first, reminding students and recording any "slips" will usually assist in suppressing those words. Systematic reinforcement of success will make the replacement words more probable. If those "forbidden" words are acceptable outside of school, improvement will take longer.

Should there not be appropriate improvement (don't expect overnight miracles) removal from situations (breaks, games) which trigger unacceptable language is appropriate. Gradual return to those situations (last five minutes of break and when that period is successful, ten minutes, increasing as the student demonstrates control) can reinforce and accelerate progress. Violations return the student to the original five minutes which, when successful, earn ten minutes, then fifteen. In other words, violations "cost" more than they are worth. If the student has earned a long break with friends, a violation that results in his/her "starting over" is more costly than a small penalty and therefore to be avoided.

Obviously, when inappropriate language is part of a students' out-of-school culture and is practiced at home and with friends, it will be more difficult to change but it can be done. You and I use different words when we shut our finger in the drawer at school and at home. Students can also learn to monitor their language accordingly.

Letting a student know how well (s)he is doing by showing the tangible evidence of a record gives knowledge of results that acts as an excellent motivator for additional improvement. Remember, in dieting, you exert more self control as you see the pounds drop off. Students need to see tangible evidence of progress in behavior as well as in academic work. Seeing progress increases motivation.

Now let's learn how we may involve parents in a team effort to help students become self disciplined.

CHAPTER X
MAKING PARENTS COLLABORATORS*

Writing a letter to the parents of a child who is having disciplinary problems can be one of the most unwelcome tasks a principal or teacher faces. Beyond the fact that no one wants to be the bearer of unwelcome tidings, there is a strong potential here for turning parents into adversaries at a time when we crucially need them as collaborators in achieving the mutually desired goal of a self controlled, successful learner.

Children are parents' most vulnerable spot. When their child misbehaves or is failing to make appropriate progress, parents may assume (often incorrectly) that they are to blame. Thus, any indication of failure on the part of the student may be interpreted by parents as their own failure.

Understandably, parents want to believe in and support their children. So when students deny guilt or disclaim responsibility, parents are prone to accept what their children say. Should the school send home word that Jim is not finishing his work, Jim will very probably attempt to convince his parents that the problem lies in the impossibility of the assignment or the lack of adequate time — not in Jim's failure to exert the necessary effort.

When Mary influences other girls in an undesirable way, Mary will argue that she is not responsible for how other students behave, and mother will not be hard to convince.

When Ralph gets into trouble on the bus, he has a believable alibi — the other kids shoved him into the bus driver and he got all the blame.

Believing one's own child is a natural, not to mention desirable, trait; and youngsters are not above capitalizing on such faith to try to drive a wedge between school and home so as not to be confronted by an alliance of those two powerful forces when students have done something "out of line."

Successful principals and teachers seek to avoid this schism between home and school by doing everything possible to resolve the issue before bringing it to parents' attention. If their effort is successful they are then in a position to send a message the parents will welcome — one complimenting the student's achievement.

Sometimes, however, the effort fails. Then it becomes the school's responsibility to notify parents of an unproductive situation and seek to enlist their support. If this communication is to result in a relationship that

* The content of this chapter originally appeared in *Here's How*. National Association of Elementary School Principals, Vol. 5, 1986.

is collaborative rather than adversarial, it must contain four important messages: *"(S)he can. But doesn't. You care. Let's plan."*

"(S)HE CAN"

We would not expect students to accomplish something unless we had evidence that they were capable of doing so (We would not expect a student with poor eye-hand coordination to complete a neat writing assignment in record speed). Parents need to receive such evidence of ability. Otherwise, they may very well draw the conclusion that the school believes their child lacks the ability to do what is expected of "normal" students, an unpleasant proposition for any parent to confront.

"BUT DOESN'T"

Parents also need to receive this information with evidence in language that deals with specific student behavior, *not* labels ("lazy," "deceitful," "irresponsible," "disrespectful," and the like). We need to communicate what students do or do not *do;* not what they supposedly *are.* Whenever possible, the message should dignify the student's behavior by stating that we understand how it could happen. "He was having so much fun with his friends..." "She is just learning how to lead..." "We are puzzled by..." In any case, such labels as "unmotivated," "immature," "rude," and the like, are to be strictly avoided, along with those often pejorative words "problem" and "concern." These are "red flag" words that arouse parents' resistance. "My child certainly is not!" the parent instinctively declares.

"YOU CARE"

Parents frequently feel that the school believes they are indifferent or unconcerned — that, "If you cared, (s)he wouldn't behave that way." Parents would never choose that their child be unsuccessful or disobedient or disrespectful. Sometimes, a few parents may throw up their hands with a difficult child, or be unable to deal with the situation, or not want to take time, or to run away from it, but they all *care.* Such parents need to be assured that the school knows full well that they care as much as we do (and probably more!) and that we appreciate their desire to help improve the situation.

"LET'S PLAN"

When we seek to enlist parents as highly valued colleagues to join in a mutual effort to increase their child's success at school, most of them (not all; a perfect record is seldom achieved in any profession) become willing collaborators. Usually, parents who avoid working with the school do so because they feel they will be "put down," thought of as inadequate, or "lectured." More than one parent has in effect declared, "I'm sick of being told I'm a bad mother." And when challenged by, "Is that what the principal (teacher) told you?" the typical response is, "No, but that's what (s)he meant."

In any case, those four messages "(S)he can, but doesn't. You care — let's plan." should become the structure around which every disciplinary communication is built.

The most welcome of the four, and thus the two that are most likely to lead to collaborative relationships, are "(S)he can" and "You care."

One of them, therefore, should be the first idea communicated by the letter. It would be really unusual that parents would discredit a message that begins with an affirmation of their child's adequacy (and thus their own).

The communication should end with the invitation to work together — "Let's plan." A definite time should be proposed for a meeting, with the alternative, "If this time is not possible for you, please telephone tomorrow morning so that we may arrange to get together as soon as possible."

Notice that the principal (or teacher) does not ask, "Will you please meet with us?" because the school does not intend to take "No" for an answer. The school truly wants to form a partnership in this venture and will not easily be turned aside.

Following are some sample letters. Note the presence of the four key components: "(S)he can, but doesn't. You care, let's plan," and observe how the letter is careful to dignify the student: "She doesn't realize...," rather than implying that she is "bad."

Dear _____ ,

Tom has shown us what good thinking he can do. He figures out very difficult problems and can support his answers.

This makes it all the more puzzling that he doesn't finish work we know he can do. As a result, we are worried that he may get behind in his studies.

We know your family really values education and plans for Tom to attend college.

So that together we can make sure he is well prepared, please meet with us at school on _____ to identify ways we can work together to assure that Tom's work matches his intellectual ability.

Should that time not be possible for you, please telephone first thing tomorrow morning so we may set a meeting time as soon as possible.

Sincerely,

Notice we are "puzzled"; we do not speak of his "problem." We say he "may get behind," not that he is behind (he may not be!) or that his case is becoming hopeless.

Dear _____ ,

We continue to be grateful for the time and ideas you have contributed to our school safety committee. Largely as a result of your group's input, our students are safer at school and more careful on the way to and from school.

We know that you want John to follow safety rules, and at school he does so very well. On the bus, however, he and his friends have so much fun together that safety gets forgotten.

Please talk to John about this matter so that he learns from you as well as from us that rules must be obeyed if he is to continue to ride the bus.

Thank you very much for your help. We feel sure we soon can let you know that he is doing just as good a job on the bus as he is at school.

Sincerely,

Consider how you would feel as a parent if you received a letter such as the following:

Dear _____ ,

Mary is constantly getting the other girls in trouble because they do whatever she tells them.

You need to come to school on _____ so we can straighten out this problem.

Sincerely,

Your feelings probably would be different if, instead, You received this letter:

Dear _____ ,

Mary has a great deal of leadership ability and the girls follow her willingly. When she helps them become more productive, everybody admires her.

When one is first learning to be a leader, it is tempting to use that power, so Mary sometimes leads others in ways that may not work out well for them.

We know that you, as we, want Mary to lead others in a way that we'll all be proud of her. Please come to school on _____ to help us enable Mary to see the difference between productive and non-productive leadership.

Sincerely,

Notice that Mary is a "beginning" leader who is "tempted," not that she is a "bad girl."

The vocabulary used in such letters may need to be adjusted for parent understanding. The same message can be given to less verbally sophisticated parents by something like the following:

Dear _____ ,

The girls all respect and admire Mary, and they want to be like her. As a result, she needs to be careful that what she does sets a good example for others.

Sometimes, Mary encourages girls to do things that you and we would not think are best, so we need to meet with you on _____ to plan ways to help Mary see the difference between helpful things and those that are hurtful to others.

Sincerely,

Students not being punctual or prepared is a common problem. A note such as the following will go a long way in eliciting parents' collaboration.

Dear _____ ,

As the leader of her group, Sara has shown that she can plan carefully. She organizes materials, time, and classmates very successfully.

In more routine matters such as being on time and bringing necessary materials to class, she frequently forgets to use her good planning ability.

We know you want Sara to be punctual and prepared so she is successful in school and in life. Please meet with us on _____ so, together, we can plan ways for Sara to extend her skills to all aspects of schooling. We know she can do it!

Sincerely,

After meeting with parents, the principal or teacher has an obligation to set a time when parents will be informed about "how things worked out"; so that they are aware that the situation has been resolved and that their contribution was importantly responsible. If the plan was not effective, at least you both know what will not work and, as collaborators, can proceed from there to make new plans that have higher probability of success.

Working together, home and school constitute a powerful team as they focus on their common goal of making students successful.

That's not likely to happen, however, unless we communicate with parents in ways that make them feel appreciated, valued, and welcome as collaborators.

CHAPTER XI
ARE YOUR WORDS "THINK STARTERS" OR "THINK STOPPERS"*

The words you use can be powerful determiners of a student's self discipline and depth of thinking. Those words can be "think stoppers" or become "think starters" which produce responsible, self directed students rather than "robots" who wait to be told what to do.

Some words stimulate thinking, others eliminate the need for it. "Put your paper in your desk" requires only that the student process a simple direction and follow it. But, when you say, "The bell is about to ring. Think about what you need to do before you're ready to be excused." this communication requires much more complex intellectual processing and places students in charge of their actions and the consequences of those actions. Instead of simply following directions, students must determine what to do and then direct themselves to do it.

There is no questions that at times, specific and unmistakable directives from the teacher are needed. Issues of safety must be speedily and effectively resolved. Most of the time, however, a teacher can deliberately select words that not only encourage thinking on the part of the student but indicate the expectation for productive self direction. Rather than being directive, "Put a period there," which actually encourages student dependence on being told what to do, your words can become "indirective" indicators that suggest thinking on the part of the student is not only needed but expected. "What do you need to do before the punctuation is just right?" promotes active thinking which results in self direction.

"Indirective" words do not tell students what to do, but indicate the situation where they need to make decisions followed by action. Your words may be questions such as, "What things do you need to check so your paper is as correct as you can make it?" *Indirective* words also can be statements which give information and stimulate the student to think further. "Your punctuation needs correcting, check the second paragraph."

Indirective communication supplies a student with information related to a given situation, task, or activity which that student needs to determine how to modify. Information should be (1) specific and / or descriptive, (2) at the student's level of understanding, and (3) require that the student have

---

* The content of this chapter originally appeared as an article co-authored by Pam Ballis in *Learning Magazine*, August 1985.

the responsibility/opportunity to make productive decisions based on the situation, his/her own knowledge, and the information received. For example, "The wind from outside is blowing our papers," requires the student to consider an undesirable situation and create a solution. This expectation for proactive thinking with resultant action is in contrast to a student's passive, reactive role when the adult uses directive communication. "Close the door."

Occasionally, we meet a "so what" student and indirective communication doesn't work. Adding the indirective statement, "Do you need help from me or can you take care of it yourself?" often supplies the stimulus that may cause the "non thinker" to think. If not, the teacher is the responsible person in charge and a direct command is not out of order.

In most cases, students who receive precise or descriptive information are able to use it as a stimulus to start their own thinking and action processes. Their subsequent feeling of being in charge of their decisions plus their resultant independence usually are much more satisfying to them (and to their teachers!). Successful self direction builds self esteem.

When you see that a student needs to do responsible thinking and decision making, try the following strategy:

1. Present a descriptive or informative statement about the situation to the student. "It's almost time for break."

2. If the student does not respond appropriately, ask a question. "What do you need to do to get ready for the break?" The student may answer but still not do it.

3. Offer alternatives. "Can you get ready by yourself or would you like (do you need) some help from me?"

As a teacher, you should select the words you are using so they become less directive. Oops! We should say, "Think of some ways you can use the information from this chapter to make your words become "think starters" rather than "think stoppers" and consequently produce thinking, self-disciplined students.

Check your understanding of the differences in the following examples:

Classroom Situation	"Think Stoppers"	"Think Starters"
You're working with a small group of students; other students are too noisy.	"Be quiet. You're making too much noise." What can you do to help us?"	"Your noise is making it hard for us to hear.
It's classroom clean-up time.	"Put the materials in the box; wipe the table with a sponge; push in the chairs."	"It's time to clean up the room. What do you need to do to make it the way it was before we started?"

Classroom Situation	"Think Stoppers"	"Think Starters"
One student is distracting another.	"Richard, move away from Kim."	"Richard, select a place where you can do a responsible job of working."
One student is making disruptive noises while another is trying to speak.	"Be quiet."	"It's Mary's turn to talk. What do you need to do?"
A student volunteers to help you.	"Get six jars of paste, six sheets of paper, and some newspaper. Pass out the paste and paper to each student at the table. Cover the table with the newspaper."	"Everyone will need paste and paper, and the table will need to be protected."
A student is whining.	"Stop whining."	"I can understand you better if you talk in your regular voice."
A student interrupts while you're talking to another student.	"Don't interrupt."	"I'm talking to Jean. If what you have to say is too important to wait, how can you get our attention politely?"
Students are fighting — hitting each other.	"Stop it! Each of you go to opposite sides of the room."	"We can't have fighting and hitting. What else could you do to let someone know you're very angry with him?"
A student forgets to put his name on his work.	"Remember to write your name on your work.	"How will we know this belongs to you?"
Students are noisy in the hallways.	"Keep quiet in the hallways."	"Students in the classrooms are trying to work. What can you do so you don't disturb them?"

Classroom Situation	Directive Communication	Indirective Communication
A student is running in the hallway.	"No running in the hallway."	"There's a reason to walk in the hallway. Can you say the reason?"
A student who can't figure out how to do something says, "I can't do this."	"Here's how to do it: First you... "	"What have you done so far? Which part is giving you trouble?"
Student leaves work around — forgets to clean up.	"Put your _____ away."	Decide where to put your _____ so you'll remember where it is when you need it?"
Student is pulling on the basketball net.	"Don't pull on the net."	"What do you need to remember about the net?"
Students are wandering around the room.	"Take your seat."	"Where should you be?"

CHAPTER XII
TEACHERS AS MODELS

Observational learning (learning by observing others do something) is a very powerful way of acquiring attitudes, skills, and knowledge. Many of our attitudes, mannerisms, speech patterns, and prejudices are learned without any intent on our part to do so, from watching "significant others" display those behaviors. Consequently, when a teacher demonstrates respect for the dignity of students and other school personnel, students are more apt to acquire that behavior. Saying, in response to a rude remark, "Have I unintentionally been rude to you? Then help me to understand why you are angry," often will diffuse what could become a hostile situation. We also need to be aware that what might appear to be rude or hostile to one person may not have been intended by the other. Questioning, *sincerely,* whether the effect was intended usually surprises an angry student and helps him/ her rephrase the hostile response.

Occasionally, we "take the bait," misinterpret what happened, or act without taking time to think — in other words, we "blow it" professionally. This can happen to all of us, however, the more professional skill we have, the less it happens.

When it does happen, the professional remediation is to acknowledge it, first to ourselves, resisting the temptation to defend our egos by justifying our behavior. Then, we need to make necessary amends, such as, "I'm sorry I blew my top at you, Alice. I didn't realize that _____ ," or "I found I was mistaken about _____ ", or "I now know that you were not involved", or "I must have been tired to have made such a big issue of _____ . I apologize."

Students will respect the mature behavior of taking responsibility for one's actions. You will become a model for *their* observational learning of more mature behavior when, in the future, they also occasionally "blow it" — something inevitable for a human being.

The way a teacher responds to a student's incorrect answer by supplying the question to which that answer really belongs, giving a prompt so that a student can respond with the correct answer, then holding the student accountable for remembering that answer in the future, clearly dignifies the student as one who is competent to give the correct answer. This type of teacher response models respect for students and discourages classmates' derision for errors. Unfortunately, the statement, "Who can help Tom?" models the opposite. That response gives the message that Tom is "dumber" than his age mates and the other students will treat him accordingly. Making clear that discourtesy to others is not acceptable in your classroom (and it must not be!) is more believable if you model it yourself.

Listening to and making sure you understand a student's point of view, even if you don't agree with it, models respect for all points of view. "Practice what you preach" also goes for teachers.

Any strategy which makes a student's undesirable behavior public knowledge is suspect. Recording an errant student's name on the board for all to see, public changing of the color of cards by a student's name to show infractions, public listing of missing assignments, moving markers on "ladders of good behavior," or giving chits or stickers may, when nothing else has worked, be a desperate attempt to start students toward improved behavior. The concurrent negative potential of those strategies which accentuate the negative rather than the positive, or using non-related punishments should cause such strategies to be dropped as soon as possible. The obsolete practice of having students write lines ("I will come to school on time,") as a punishment is usually useless and corporal punishment has no place in an effective school.

Inevitably, the question arises, "Should the group be punished for the misbehavior of a few?" Usually, the answer is, "No, each person should accept the consequences for his / her own behavior." The world, however, does not always function that way. You and I pay higher insurance rates because of other's carelessness, higher medical rates because of malpractice suits. Sometimes we do have to accept responsibility and consequences for other's behavior. Professionals take on the monitoring and discipline of their fellow professionals. Sometimes classes should do the same.

Occasionally, by making the group responsible for all group members' behavior, needed social pressure is exerted on a few. We need to be careful, however, that we are not perceived as unfair or those few are not so alienated or rejected as a result of the pressure that a result occurs which is opposite to what we intended. Being able to spoil it for the group can give a few individuals a great deal of power that they may use in retaliation for group disapproval. This is one more example of the necessity for teacher judgment in *this* situation with *these* students. There are no absolute rules. An "advanced degree in wizardry" is needed by the teacher.

Usually, a more effective strategy is to divide "sinners" into two matched groups and have those groups compete in achieving more desirable behaviors with resultant reinforcers. Competition is healthy only if both sides have a chance to win.

Another effective strategy is to have individuals compete against their own past records with growth being recorded, recognized, and rewarded.

If you have lotteries for ''good behavior tickets,'' they should be weighted in favor of students who need it and against those few who, with little effort, might profit from such a system. Unfortunately, even if it works, there is little or no transfer to new situations where there is not a lottery.

Remember, there are no ''always right'' answers in the complex profession of education. As you make wise, just, discipline decisions which are sensitive to the needs of each student, which reflect your professional knowledge, and which you implement artistically, you become an important model who students will emulate.

As you ''keep your cool'' when a student is trying to get you to react, as you understand that for some students, self control may be difficult at times, as you judge behavior rather than the student, as you systematically and artistically use professional knowledge to solve discipline problems, as you are fair, just, and understanding of others, you are modeling qualities that can be acquired by observational learning. Students will not only respect you, they will learn those behaviors from one of their most ''significant others.''

As you are critically aware, discipline decisions are not based on impulse, instinct, or tradition if those decisions are to develop self discipline, responsible, contributing, happy students. All decisions in teaching, whether academic or disciplinary, should be made carefully, deliberately (even when made at high speed), based on research and implemented with artistry.

Using this book as a source of guidance will assist you on your way to becoming the superb professional you have the potential for being. In turn, your skills will enable students to become ''their very best selves.''

Students whom you help to become self disciplined and thereby self actualized will make your influence on this world never ending. That is why education is the most important profession of all.

CHAPTER XIII
A TEACHER'S RESPONSE*

Has my definition of discipline changed as a result of this book? Yes, and no.

"Yes," in that I now realize that I am "disciplining" even when I am not keeping students in order. When I am helping them develop their own inner self-mastery, when I help them see the need for or reason for them to monitor and be responsible for their own actions, when teacher and pupil work together to achieve a common goal, that is the ultimate form of discipline. Those moments of important, subtle contact between a student and me with a resulting freeing of creative energy for both of us, that is the highest form of discipline.

"No," in that account should be taken of the equally valid fact that students sometimes "get the devil in them." They have destructive as well as constructive impulses and needs. A teacher can work on one level with a child who is in a serious, "good" frame of mind. But when that student arrives at school with a reckless gleam in his eye and a curl to his lip, or with an almost visible black cloud over her head because of some self-demeaning experience with a significant adult that morning, than watch out! At that time, they will not cooperate with the teacher or discuss their own behavior to make it more productive for themselves and others. Their minds have closed, emotions run rampant. They are primed for disruption and glory in violence. This is no time for gentle reasoning from the teacher but is an appropriate time for authoritarian firmness, gently if possible, but if not, strongly.

When the rain is coming, or the wind is blowing wildly and students act as if they had been plugged into electrical sockets, with "nice" little girls suddenly transformed into screaming monsters, the time has come to say, strongly, "Everybody stop and look at me!" They do so; a blessed peace (the eye of the hurricane) falls upon the room. The students are glad that you are holding the reins tightly. They subconsciously know that they cannot control themselves and are afraid of their own wildness.

It is very interesting that a college teacher with whom I discussed this type of day didn't know what I was talking about. No, he didn't see any difference between the behavior of students the week before Christmas or

---

* Written by Dorthy Horner, Santa Monica Teacher

125

the last days of school before summer vacation. It wasn't a time of horror for him, leaving him exhausted, hating the sight or sound of students. But all the public school teachers I have ever talked to reacted as if I had pushed an only too familiar emotional teaching button. Young children seem to be much more at the mercy of their feelings than are high school or college students who have learned to conceal if not control their emotions. I don't suppose many college professors have ever seen, as I have, a docile, sweet, gentle child simply clench her fists, jump up and down, and scream for no other reason than that she had been infected with group hysteria.

Perhaps many of us in classrooms would take the pronouncements of educators about discipline much more seriously if professors gave any indication of having lived through some of the wild days described above, with children obviously beyond their own ability to control themselves.

I have watched myself carefully during these last weeks as a result of reading this book, and have come to some definite conclusions (revelations?) about myself as a disciplinarian.

First: When I am in top physical shape I can "discipline" in a way that takes into account the whole child, his total needs as well as the situation of the moment, in a "No-Win No-Lose" manner which leaves both the student and me satisfied and pleased with ourselves. I can tell this from my own feelings and from the student's expression and subsequent behavior of being in charge of self.

Second: When I am not feeling well or am dazed with allergies or lack of sleep, I simply cannot handle the subtle nuances of a situation — I am not really aware of them — and my "discipline" is more rough and primitive with a residue of dissatisfaction for both the child and me. I don't do terrible things to the child, but my pride is hurt that I didn't do the kind of job of which I know I am capable.

Third: As I have noted above, there are occasions for sharp, drill sergeant tactics. ("Go to your seats! Open your books to page 16. Be ready to answer the first question.") Since my real definition for discipline is to do for the student what is needed at the time, it is obvious to me that different student needs call for different teacher reactions. To me, it is stupid to be a "gentleman in a jungle," for it is a denial of reality, a seeing of a tiger as not a tiger but as a gentle puppy. And granted the "tiger" has the capability to change into a "puppy," you wait till the tiger has receded before you use subtlety on the puppy.

I have long been an admirer of high level professional aims and practices. Watching expert teachers in action is growth evoking and inspirational. Each time I see a teacher applying discipline that develops student's self-discipline in a classroom situation, I find something else to upgrade my own teaching. For example, the way one teacher dismissed the students from the

126

group to their learning tasks was an absolute revelation. Having students "tell themselves" what they needed to do improved my clean-up periods unbelievably. Based, as it is, on the proposition that students need to call to their conscious mind just what they are going to do, and how, before they begin, to direct themselves, stops most of that aimless wandering and time wasting. I now get a verbal commitment from students before I release them to begin. I even passed this technique on to our school librarian who was at her wits end because of children aimlessly roaming the library during their class visit. She now sits each class down when they enter, gets a verbal commitment from each child about how (s)he will use the facilities, and direct self. Then peace and quiet reigns. Everybody is productively busy and students are "self disciplined."

Another most valuable learning was the use of a private reminder or individual conference. I used it on Leslie, a restless, incessantly talking girl who couldn't settle down to work. Together we planned that her need to talk, and my need that all students in my room have the opportunity to grow and learn, could be resolved by her electing to sit in a different place during work periods. It worked with no hard feelings.

I am trying to keep this, "You're in charge of your own behavior" attitude in mind as I deal with students and also never, never to begin an accusatory sentence with "You." I used these techniques with Greg, child of divorced parents, filled with self-hate. His problem is the same as Leslie's. We are now on friendly terms and his work is beginning to be legible and neat. He is becoming proud of his accomplishments and happily takes home "good" notes to his mother.

As for resolving my concerns about discipline, I have found no other solution than to walk a precarious tightrope between the needs of the students and those of the school, being as much of a human being, as well as a teacher, as possible, pulling myself back when I lean too much one way or the other, which none of us can help doing as imperfect mortals. My own self-discipline will help!

REINFORCEMENT THEORY
SELF TEST

If you wish to give yourself some positive (we hope) reinforcement by knowing how much you have learned, take this test.

Let us assume you have decided to train your group of boys and girls to stop whatever they are doing and look at you when you give some pre-arranged signal (If you have not decided this with every group of students you teach, you had better start now).

1. You will need to give the signal and:

    a. have them show others how well they can do it
    b. punish those who do not respond
    c. give them practice
    d. praise those who do it well
    e. explain it again

2. At first you will need to:

    a. praise them every time they respond well
    b. praise them every other time they respond well
    c. praise them at irregular times
    d. punish those who do not respond every time
    e. punish those who do not respond at irregular times

3. If you praise the students who look up at the signal and ignore those who do not, you are attempting to:

    a. negatively reinforce
    b. give practice
    c. switch to an intermittent schedule of reinforcement
    d. use a regular schedule of reinforcement
    e. extinguish the response of not looking up

4. If you negatively reinforce students who do not look up at the signal, it means:

   a. you want the children to know you mean business
   b. you want to identify the non-conformers
   c. you think ignoring the offenders will not make the behavior disappear
   d. children need to know the consequences of their acts
   e. you think misbehavior should be punished

5. If you punish a student who does not respond to the signal, it means you:

   a. want children to know you are aware of those who do not look at you
   b. want to suppress his ''not looking at you''
   c. want to shape his behavior
   d. want to be fair to the other children who always look at you
   e. are alert to the identification of children who have not yet learned the behavior

6. If possible, you should avoid punishment because:

   a. a positive approach is always better
   b. it isn't very effective
   c. it won't extinguish a response
   d. it may have undesirable side-effects
   e. children will resent it

7. In order to be sure students do not easily forget their response to the signal, you will need to:

   a. remind them often
   b. punish those who forget
   c. switch to an intermittent schedule where you praise them occasionally
   d. give them lots of practice
   e. use a regular schedule where you praise them every time

8. If you wish to change behavior, it is essential that you know that punishment:

   a. will not extinguish a response
   b. is a negative approach
   c. gives children a wrong impression of the teacher
   d. is sometimes necessary
   e. will not shape behavior

9. Johnny is talking and the teacher frowns at him. He stops and once again she looks pleasant. His response of not talking has been strengthened because:

   a. it took away the frown
   b. the class has noticed the teacher frowning at him
   c. the teacher my report his behavior to his mother
   d. the frown reminds him of the "no talking" rule
   e. talking got him in trouble

10. Saying "be careful when you work" is not reinforcement because:

    a. it is not positive
    b. it does not follow a response
    c. it may not be needed
    d. it is not appropriate for all children
    e. children should remember it themselves

11. When Jim picks up paper on the yard, the teacher praises him. Her praise should be:

    a. reinforcement
    b. identification of behavior
    c. positive reinforcement
    d. a regular schedule of reinforcement
    e. an intermittent schedule of reinforcement

12. The students come into the room with the teacher watching. She says they are acting very grown up when they take out their spelling books. They study quietly and get ready for their spelling test. Which behavior is the most likely to reoccur?

    a. coming in quietly
    b. taking out their spelling books
    c. study quietly
    d. get ready for the test
    e. all of these

13. Ignoring a student's undesirable behavior should indicate the teacher:

    a. feels she should not make too much of it
    b. can't pay attention to everything
    c. has not seen it
    d. wishes to extinguish the behavior
    e. feels negative reinforcement is inappropriate

14. In order for behavior to be resistant to forgetting, a teacher must:

    a. positively reinforce it every time it occurs
    b. positively reinforce it every other time it occurs
    c. positively reinforce it intermittently
    d. positively reinforce differently for different problems
    e. positively reinforce differently for different children

15. When a teacher wishes a student to learn a new response as quickly as possible, she should use:

    a. positive reinforcement
    b. negative reinforcement
    c. extinction
    d. a continuous schedule of positive reinforcement
    e. an intermittent schedule of positive reinforcement

16. A teacher tells a student he must stop being a poor sport and she will punish him if the behavior continues. Her major error has been:
    a. using negative reinforcement
    b. not using positive reinforcement
    c. identifying the undesirable behavior
    d. not identifying the desirable behavior
    e. conditioning him against sports

17. Bob never listens to instuctions. After they are given, he always asks a dozen unnecessary questions. You do not wish to discourage valid questions, but you think he should develop the ability to attend well enough so he will need to ask only about areas not covered in the instructions. As Bob begins to listen carefully to instructions, you will need to:

a. praise him every time
b. praise him every other time
c. praise him at the times it seems appropriate
d. punish children who don't listen every time
e. occasionally punish children who do not listen

18. If you praise Bob's good questions and ignore his foolish ones, it is because you:

a. are accentuating the positive
b. believe that by praising the good ones, the poor ones will disappear
c. don't wish to humiliate him in front of the group
d. it sets an example for others
e. wish him to build self confidence

19. You have decided to praise Bob for asking good questions because:

a. it shows he is really thinking
b. he had to hear the instructions in order to frame a good question
c. it's important that children feel free to ask questions
d. it sets an example for others
e. he needs to know you are not picking on him

20. After Bob has learned to listen well and you praise him only occasionally for listening and following directions you are:

a. making sure the other children don't feel slighted
b. being a normal hum being who does not always remember
c. feeling he should be able to go on his own
d. making sure his listening will continue even if you are not the teacher
e. ready to move on to his next learning task

Correct answers

1—d	6—d	11—c	16—d
2—a	7—c	12—b	17—a
3—e	8—a	13—d	18—b
4—c	9—a	14—c	19—b
5—b	10—b	15—d	20—d

If you have more than 15 correct –

You're a whiz! (positive reinforcement)

If you have 7-14 correct –

You're doing okay, but you may need to review parts of this book so you will increase you success in the classroom.

If you have less than 7 correct –

Shame on us! (negative reinforcement) Turn back to page one and if you still don't get it, write us a letter so we can revise this book.